BEFORE I FORGET
Directing Television: 1948-1988

James Sheldon

Before I Forget — Directing Television: 1948-1988
© 2011 James Sheldon. All Rights Reserved.

No part of this book may be reproduced in any form or by any means, electronic, mechanical, digital, photocopying or recording, except for the inclusion in a review, without permission in writing from the publisher.

Published in the USA by:
BearManor Media
PO Box 1129
Duncan, Oklahoma 73534-1129
www.bearmanormedia.com

ISBN 978-1-59393-639-6

Printed in the United States of America.
Book design by Brian Pearce | Red Jacket Press.

Table of Contents

Foreword by Ron Simon, *Curator, The Paley Center for Media* 5

Acknowledgements 9

Prologue 11

CHAPTER 1: *We, the People:* Commercial Television Begins........17

CHAPTER 2: *Holiday Hotel* to *Mister Peepers:* More Sets In Use.....35

CHAPTER 3: *Studio One* and *Robert Montgomery Presents:*
The Golden Age of Television 45

CHAPTER 4: *Bus Stop:* Learning From the Master 57

CHAPTER 5: How I Got Started: A Look Back 61

CHAPTER 6: CBS, Hollywood: The Move West and Live to Film....71

CHAPTER 7: *The Millionaire, The Donna Reed Show* and
Death Valley Days: Dramas, Comedies and Westerns..............81

CHAPTER 8: *The Twilight Zone, The Fugitive* and *Route 66:*
Me and Television At Our Best 91

CHAPTER 9: *The Bing Crosby Show, Family Affair*
and *My Three Sons:* Networks Take Control 107

CHAPTER 10: *Sanford & Son, M*A*S*H* and *Love Boat:*
Ratings Soar But the Fun Is Gone............................... 125

CHAPTER 11: *Cagney & Lacey, The Dukes of Hazzard*
and *The Equalizer:* Lots of Cops, Lots of Robbers 137

Epilogue 151

Appendix.. 155

Index 161

Foreword
by Ron Simon
Curator, The Paley Center for Media

James Sheldon is one of the true gentlemen in the television industry. His imagination and intelligence strike you as soon as you meet him. I have had the privilege of knowing Jim for many years, a friendship I dearly prize. He has been a major supporter of the Paley Center for Media, where I am Curator of radio and television. It was an honor to interview him about his career and accomplishments during an eventful evening at the Film Forum in March 2006; the audience savored his every wise word. But I never knew the full range and diversity of Jim's directorial work until I read this engrossing autobiography.

I have read many personal accounts about the creative development of television over its first fifty years, but most books lack a wider scope. The stories focus exclusively on the years of live television or comedy in the seventies. I can't think of another director who was there at the beginning as television took off as a mass medium in the late forties and then stayed with the medium throughout its artistic evolution for more than five decades. Jim not only helped to formulate the grammar of television, but also sustained the medium through its growth pangs and later dominance as America's favorite entertainment.

We see in Jim's story how TV developed from a live theatrical medium, produced mostly on the East Coast, to a popular storyteller, based on the generic formulas of Hollywood. Jim's talent was such that he could be embraced by almost every format. The breadth of genres he directed is almost staggering (and I have only given a few titles in each category!): live drama (*Studio One*, *Armstrong Circle Theatre*); live comedy (*Mr. Peepers*); musicals (*Holiday Hotel*, *Paul Whiteman's Goodyear Revue*); situation comedy (*My Three Sons*, *Sanford and Son*, *That Girl*); westerns (*Wagon Train*, *Gunsmoke*, *The Virginian*); detective (*Richard Diamond*, *The

Equalizer); police (*Naked City, Ironsides, Cagney & Lacey*); children's (*Walt Disney's Wonderful World of Color*); family (*The Waltons, James at 15, Family*); military (*West Point Story, M*A*S*H*); soap opera (*Knots Landing*); rural (*Petticoat Junction, The Dukes of Hazzard*); spy (*The Man from U.N.C.L.E*); comic strip (*Batman*); legal (*Perry Mason, Owen Marshall, Counselor at Law*); medical (*Doc Elliot, Nurse*); suspense (*Alfred Hitchcock Presents, The Fugitive*); education (*Room 222*); romance (*Love, American Style, The Love Boat*); fantasy (*The Twilight Zone*); and adventure (*Route 66*). Can you conceive of a man with the curiosity, intellect, and aptitude to understand the rhythms and aesthetic requirements of so many genres? His name is James Sheldon.

Jim is great to play the game of "Six Degrees of Separation" because he has directed practically everybody: Paul Newman, James Dean, Dustin Hoffman, Bing Crosby, Rock Hudson, Lee Remick, Diahann Carroll, and even an automobile in the infamous *My Mother The Car*. This memoir has so many great stories about working with actors that I won't give away any more names.

I can think of no better way of learning the history of television than hearing the life story of James Sheldon. Jim, thank you for remembering.

Acknowledgements

A few years ago, writer Jim Rosin interviewed me for his book on *Route 66*. He knew I had directed several episodes and asked if I had any pictures. I did. I also had stories. Then he did a book on *Naked City* and I helped out with more stories and more pictures. He has more than returned the favor by introducing me to the people at Bear Manor Media, who are now publishing this book. Thanks are also due to writer Stephen Bowie for his research and help and to Elaine Spooner, now at Warner Brothers, for inviting me to speak at the Creative Writers Conference in Portland, Oregon where *Before I Forget* really began. A big thanks to Stephen and Joy Schary Kabak who were there cheering me on. To Stanley Newman, Bruce Goldstein, Jane Scovell, Ron Simon, and Joe Gagliardi, all of whom contributed their opinions. And to actor Michael Chmiel for his invaluable editorial assistance.

James Sheldon
New York City, April 2011

Prologue

I stepped off the "1" train and walked up the stairs to Seventh Avenue, in Manhattan's Greenwich Village. Half a block down Houston Street, a long line trailed out the double doors of the movie theater and onto the sidewalk. Above the theater, in big block letters, the marquee announced, "AN EVENING WITH JAMES SHELDON." In the window of the box office, a handwritten sign read, "SOLD OUT."

Tears formed in my eyes. It was the beginning of one of the most meaningful nights of my life.

I had been to the Film Forum, one of New York's best-known cinematheques, before. I had even spoken there once. During a tribute to James Dean, when the Forum screened a pair of kinescopes from the "Golden Age" of live television, I had been invited to come and describe the experiences I had while directing Dean in those shows. But tonight, I was to be the center of attention.

I did a double take when I saw all those people milling about outside the theater. I knew that my family and many of my friends had planned to attend this tribute to my work as a director. But I thought they might be the only ones there. Many of the television shows I directed could be called classics, but I had no idea that so many people were still interested in them, or in me.

The evening began with a montage of the opening title cards of the many series for which I directed episodes. As the medley of famous theme songs played, the members of the audience realized that each of them, at some point or another, had watched something I had directed.

Bruce Goldstein, the repertory programmer for the Film Forum, introduced me to the audience. Then he turned the microphone over to Ron Simon, of the Museum of Television and Radio (now the Paley Center for Media), who would be asking me questions about my career in between the television clips he and Bruce had selected to represent my work. I sat in the front row as the scenes from *Mister Peepers* and *The Twilight Zone* and

Naked City, of James Dean and Wally Cox and Rock Hudson, unspooled on a screen bigger than any on which I had watched them before. It seemed as if my whole professional life was flickering before my eyes.

As I looked at the clips, I remembered what my life was like when I began directing television in 1948. I remembered how primitive the cameras were, and how we seemed to make everything up as we went along. In my mind, I saw the faces of the people I met on location all across the country when I directed *Route 66*. I saw the faces of my two sons when they worked as extras on *Naked City*, and then the face of the eldest, James, Jr., when he spent a season as an extra in the high school classroom of *Room 222*. James was a boy in the first show and nearly a man in the second. I felt a twinge in my back as I thought of the ligament I tore while climbing to the steep, snowy location of an episode of *West Point Story*. I felt the hard seat of my red, high-backed wooden director's chair, custom-made to compensate for the lifelong back pain I carried with me from that *West Point Story* shoot.

When the lights came up, I turned around in my seat and scanned the audience, looking for familiar faces. There were several dozen. I spotted my sons, James Jr. and Tony, and their mother, Eleanor. I noticed Stan Newman, who had been a senior executive at Universal, and Joanne Melniker Stern, a former entertainment editor at *Look* magazine who was also an old girlfriend. I saw Susan Kohner Weitz, the actress who had been nominated for an Oscar for *Imitation of Life*, and our mutual friend Orin O'Brien, the first female member of the New York Philharmonic (and the daughter of silent movie actor George O'Brien). I saw my childhood friend Roy Asch, who I had known since we were teenagers.

Another guest in the audience that night was Gloria Stroock, an actress who I had dated sixty years ago and who is still one of my best friends. Gloria's father had been the head of the Brooks Costume Company, and he had invited us to many opening nights of great Broadway shows — like the original productions of *Carousel*, *Finian's Rainbow*, and *Guys and Dolls*.

Gloria stood up and described the first time I directed her. It was in 1946, on a radio show called *Crimes of Carelessness*. This particular script was set in 1909, and Gloria played a young woman who wanted to get a job. Her father, a successful businessman, told her that a woman's place is in the home.

Gloria's line was supposed to be: "But father, you have a woman in your business — Miss So-and-So, the bookkeeper." What she actually said on air was: "But father, you have your business in a woman — Miss

So-and-So, the bookkeeper." In the control room, we fell on the floor laughing. Gloria glanced up and wondered where we'd all gone.

It was only then that Gloria realized her flub. She thought she'd never work again. She explained how grateful she'd been that I had hired her to appear on the show again the following week.

After two hours of film clips, I stood and took questions, first from

JS at Portland Creative Writing Conference.

Ron Simon and then from members of the audience. I felt a charge as I talked about my experiences and felt the genuine interest of the people in the theater.

Around the same time, I made some other public appearances. I was invited to lecture at the Creative Writing Conference in Portland, Oregon. I gave a brief talk on television's history, illustrating my remarks with clips from several shows I had directed. At an event devoted to the written word, anything that incorporates moving imagery will stand out, and my presentation proved popular. One member of the audience asked, "Why don't you write a book?"

And that's how the idea was planted.

Since then, I have taken my show on the road — or rather, on the waves. After the Portland conference, a couple of cruise lines invited me to deliver my lecture to their passengers, in exchange for free passage. I chatted up the audience, dropped names, and showed scenes from television episodes I directed. Along with the anecdotes, I tried to sketch in a detailed picture of what it was like to craft an entertaining, economical story within the many technical and temporal limitations of early television.

Maybe it was just because they were a captive audience, but my shipboard friends from the Caribbean to the Mediterranean enjoyed these talks. The cruise lines kept asking me back, and over time I added more clips from my shows and digitized many of the rare photos I had carefully saved over the years. Eventually I was invited to deliver variations on these lectures at the New York Public Library and the Players Club.

But still I kept coming back to that question from the man in my first audience. Why didn't I write a book? There were good reasons not to write one. I didn't need the money. The Directors Guild of America provides me with a comfortable pension, and I still get residual payments when my most popular shows — *The Virginian, The Fugitive, M*A*S*H* — are shown all over the world, from Spain to Poland to the Netherlands.

Also, I wasn't sure if I wanted to start a new career in my eighties. Directing is a social pursuit. As a director, I was blessed with talented collaborators who constantly stimulated my creative abilities. Collaboration is the definition of a director's job. Writing would be a solitary task, much more so than the public lectures in which I first began to examine my body of work with a critic's eye. Writing this book would mean collaborating with no one except my computer.

But, in the end, as I approached my ninetieth birthday, I decided that I had to tackle this project. I remember most of the things I've done, and I wanted to set them down on paper…before I forget.

Onstage *We, the People*.

CHAPTER 1

We, the People:
Commercial Television Begins

My first television broadcast was on June 1, 1948. Even though many of my crew and I were novices and unknowns, our television debut was accorded the pomp and circumstance that might have accompanied the launch of a movie directed by Cecil B. DeMille.

"This will be an exciting premiere," read the program for the evening. "We are supplying klieg lights, limousines, fresh cement, mounted police, and all devices which can contribute to the importance of the occasion." The audience consisted entirely of invited guests, entertainers and society types, who were asked to dress in formal attire. The famous comedian Fred Allen did a routine to warm up the audience before airtime, and the president of CBS, Dr. Frank Stanton, took the stage to introduce the broadcast.

So just what occasioned all this attention? *We, the People* had been a successful radio show on CBS for fourteen years. Now, CBS had made plans to introduce *We, the People* as a live television program as well, one of the earliest to debut in what is generally considered the first full TV season of nightly prime-time programming. The network wanted to attract as much attention to the event as possible.

The opportunity to transition into television so early, at a time when even the definition of what a TV director did had not been settled, was a stroke of good fortune that came my way accidentally. I had been working in radio for a few years (more on that later) when I received a promising job offer. In the spring of 1948, Rod Erickson, my immediate boss at radio station WOR, the Mutual Broadcasting flagship station in New York, was hired by one of the top advertising agencies, Young & Rubicam, to take over producing *We, the People*. He asked me to join him as the show's new director.

(At the time, program content in radio and television was controlled more by the sponsors than by the networks. Advertising agencies often created shows to fill the blocks of airtime that they purchased for their clients, and until the 1950s it was common for those of us in radio and television to work directly for the agencies.)

We, the People was a unique mixture of both serious and light news and documentary programming, somewhat comparable to today's *60 Minutes*, but with only a single interviewer. At the time I began directing the show, Dwight Wiest filled that role. *We, the People* contained about six stories a week — a couple from current news, some from the sports world, at least one from the entertainment community. As the publicity read: "*We, the People* concerned itself primarily with real life stories told by the people who had experienced them...people from every corner of the globe."

My first segment was broadcast on April 20, 1948, and only six weeks later, CBS and the show's sponsor, Gulf Oil, decided to also air *We, the People* on television. Some popular radio shows that went on television required extensive retooling. For instance, the cast of radio's *Amos'n'Andy* were white and had to be replaced by black actors for the screen. But because *We, the People* was primarily non-fiction, CBS decided to "simulcast" (a new word at the time) the show on both radio and television at the same time. It was an economic coup for the sponsor, but still required many adjustments behind the scenes.

We, the People was being broadcast live from coast to coast from the stage of New York's Maxine Elliott Theatre. Located on the lower end of the Broadway district, on Thirty-ninth Street between Sixth and Seventh Avenues, the Maxine Elliott had been home to theater history during the preceding decades. It was the stage on which Orson Welles' historic production of *Cradle Will Rock* would have played, had not the show been shut down before its debut because of Welles' clash with the management of the Federal Theatre project. Now the Maxine Elliott housed a radio and television studio, and it would be the site of our star-studded *We, the People* premiere.

The radio version of *We, the People* had a live audience, but all they saw were the performers standing at microphones, and occasionally at a table and some chairs on the stage. For television, small sets were added for the benefit of the camera, their design determined by the subject matter of the particular interview.

Cameras were placed in the rear and on the sides of the broadcast studio. Cue cards, off camera, replaced the scripts which the participants used to hold in their hands. For the first time, the guests wore makeup, and their wardrobe was selected with the television lighting in mind. In the orchestra pit, we still had the twenty-two piece Oscar Bradley Orchestra, conducted by Emerson Buckley.

There was also a new addition to *We, the People*'s crew. The network assigned one of their top video directors, Ralph Levy, to be in charge of photographing what I staged. In the control room at the back of the theater, they added necessary equipment. During the rehearsals, Ralph

Fred Allen, Nat King Cole & Eden Abez on *We, the People*.

Levy and his assistant talked to the cameramen and cued the camera cuts.

On that first simulcast, there were very special guests. The program offered serious stories, like Mrs. Spencer Tracy talking about her deaf son and the John Tracy Clinic she had started. Fun was provided by Fred Allen, the popular radio comedian. There was someone who made the perfect steak, and a biker named Evil Eye Knievel. As a musical guest, we had Eden Abez, a bearded hippie who wrote the then-current hit song *Nature Boy*, which had been recorded by the King Cole Trio. For our show, Nat King Cole performed it live with our orchestra.

Outside the Maxine Elliott Theatre that night, crowds gathered to gape at the celebrity arrivals. Inside, as they took their seats, members of the specially invited audience were handed mimeographed notes. Like most people in 1948, they were unfamiliar with television, so we gave them instructions as to how they should conduct themselves.

With all the hoopla going on outside, those of us in the crew of *We, the People* could not help but notice that we were involved in something big. We hoped we were making history that night, but in retrospect, we had no concept of how much of an impact television was going to have on the whole world. Suddenly, I was a director in a new medium of entertainment, one in which I continued to work for another exciting forty years.

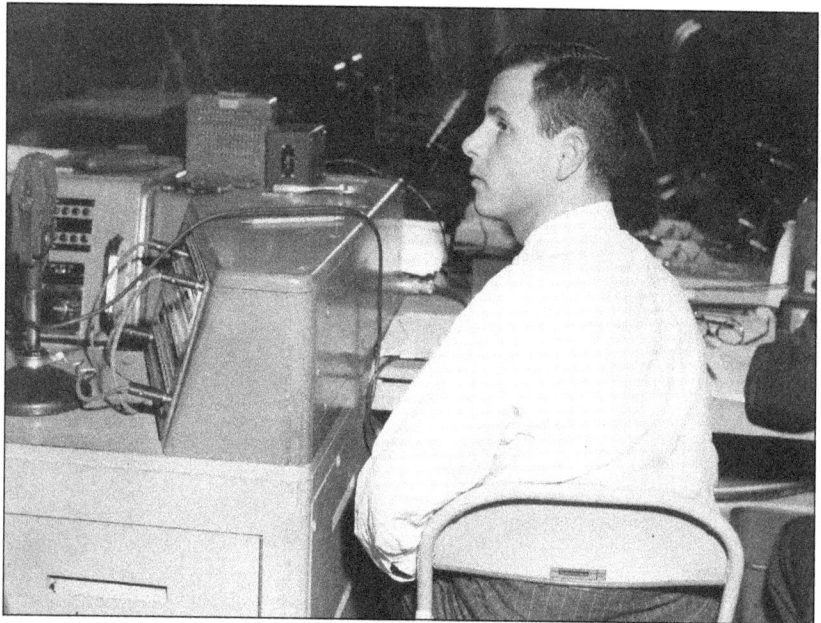

JS in the Control Room.

Even though no one had done this before, including me, I was amazingly calm and enjoyed what I was doing. Considering that we were all experimenting with something brand new, that evening went well. "*We, the People* proves its mettle," wrote the New York *World-Telegram*'s Edmond Leary.

The simulcast experiment was being watched closely by the entire radio industry. Blending the old medium with the new one presented problems, which we had to solve from week to week. Edmond Leary described a scene of chaos at 5pm on a broadcast day. "Following the dress rehearsal…in the Maxine Elliott Theater, everything seemed in such a state of hopeless confusion, a casual visitor dropping in would have bet odds the show would not have been able to go on the air four hours later," he wrote. (Actually, the activity Leary described was just the run-through which preceded our dress rehearsal.) "Lines had to be corrected, previous music cues lengthened or shortened, other changes effected. Rehearsals before the cameras had occupied most of the day…for very few of the people who appear on the program have had experience before a mic or a television camera."

Those early cameras were heavy, and had triple turret lenses which enabled the cameraman to change the size of the images. Eventually, the zoom lens made this more flexible — on-air tightening or widening became possible without moving the camera. Cameras were, of course, the most important of the new ingredients on *We, the People* after we went to television. But I learned quickly.

The CBS camera director, Ralph Levy, was very anxious to have his own show and couldn't wait to teach me all about television cameras. So I learned which was the close-up lens, and which was the wide-shot. I learned how best to move the unwieldy cables, and where the sound boom had to be. I learned how to think visually.

Soon, I assumed responsibility for both the audio and video programs, and Ralph went on to great success directing both the Jack Benny and the Burns and Allen TV shows each week.

The trade publication *Billboard* headlined a February 1949 article: "People reshuffle follows Sheldon rise." In that month, the producer of *We, the People*, Rod Erickson, moved up to supervise all programming at Young & Rubicam. Rod offered me the chance to move up the advertising echelon with him, but I chose to remain in show biz. I took the producer's chair that Rod had vacated, and a Young and Rubicam executive, Lindsay MacHarrie took on a supervisory role. Less than a year after debuting as just the radio director of *We, the People*, I was now responsible for producing and directing both the radio and television broadcasts.

Even if *We, the People*'s major audience was on the radio, I was personally much more interested in the steadily increasing number of viewers who had television sets, and in the visuals we sent out to them. For example, we had music bridges in between the different stories on radio, and originally we accompanied these transitions with just bookmark vaudeville cards on a little stand on the stage. The lovely Neva Patterson, later a successful actress on stage and in the movies, would walk out and change the card in between guests. Neva and I hit it off very well that night and a year-long romance developed. A lifelong friendship followed.

Now, for television, we needed something more elaborate than those cards. The writers and I began to come up with thematic staging ideas to segue in between guests. We used actors or dancers, and added costumes and even scenery and props, just to liven up a few seconds of transitional music. I was proud of this added bit of color, and more importantly, I now had an excuse to work with actors.

We, the People pioneered in other ways. We did remote telecasts away from our studio. That's not unusual today, but ours was one of the first shows to do it.

For one segment, on October 2, 1949, our show went to Philadelphia

Working with actors on *We, the People*.

to broadcast from a Red Cross benefit. We had an unusually good group of guests on the show that night: Harold Russell, who had lost his hands in the war and won an Academy Award for acting in *The Best Years of Our Lives*; bandleader Bob Crosby, Bing's brother; singer Ella Logan, star of the then-Broadway hit *Finian's Rainbow*; Al Capp, cartoonist and creator of *L'il Abner*; and the orchestra and glee club from the Widener School for Crippled Children. It was quite a mixture of talent and yet it came off without any noticeable hitches.

Other remote broadcasts were more challenging. We did one from New York's Madison Square Garden, with the whole program built around the Ringling Brothers — Barnum and Bailey Circus. Capturing the action of the performers as they leapt all around the vast Big Top would have been difficult under any circumstances, but this show was further complicated by the fact that I had broken my leg while skiing during my honeymoon. I had a full cast on my left leg from the foot to the hip. But with crutches, I managed to hobble around, and I discovered a surprising advantage to my condition. Though there were other programs originating from the circus that week, the clowns and acrobats all remembered "the guy on crutches" and it was easy to get them to remember my directions without getting confused. We placed extra cameras strategically around the Garden, and as I called the carefully planned shots from our improvised control room, I realized it didn't matter if mistakes were made. All the pictures were great.

Our program had a staff of eager reporters who did the interviewing and wrote the scripts. Some were there when I came, and others were people I helped to bring in. I had gone to school with Lenny Safire, whose brother was the *New York Times* correspondent William Safire. Adrian Spies was a college chum, who later became a major television writer-producer in Los Angeles. Michael Mindlin, Jr., was an ace reporter who I had known since childhood, and who later became a vice-president at Warner Bros.

The entire production staff who worked for Young and Rubicam were dedicated, and the CBS people who joined us on the rehearsal and performance day became part of the hard working *We, The People* family. Dave Berman headed the staff who transcribed the scripts onto cue cards, and Bob Blier, the stage manager, went on to become the director of the popular *Arthur Godfrey Show*. Dan Seymour, who started out announcing our commercials, eventually replaced Dwight Wiest as the show's host.

There were other times when I traveled for *We, the People* without my crew. On June 20, 1949, I received a letter from the Department of the Air Force inviting me to fly to Frankfurt to do a story on the last days of the Berlin Airlift. Berlin was still divided into four sections, with our forces stationed, obviously, in the American sector. I drove to the military airport in Massachusetts and the Air Force flew me to Frankfurt. I interviewed the officers there, then flew in the airlift helicopter to the American Sector in Berlin and interviewed more of our troops there. I recorded all of this material with my own sixteen-millimeter camera. Content on *We, the People* was always live, whether it be segments or commercials. When I returned to New York with my footage, it was shown as a special part of the airlift segment.

On a variety program like *We, the People*, the most exciting part of going to work each week was meeting the array of luminaries who appeared on the program. I directed sports figures like Gene Tunney and Jack Dempsey, Mickey Mantle and Connie Mack, along with stage stars including Mary Martin, Ezio Pinza (the opera singer who became a smash on Broadway in *South Pacific* in 1949), Wagnerian opera singers Lauritz Melchior, and Helen Traubel. I was particularly thrilled to work with Melchior, since he was the star of the first opera I ever saw. We also had old-timers like Fifi D'Orsay, the Dolly Sisters, and Gloria Swanson.

Linda Christian, Tyrone Power & JS backstage.

At first the Hollywood studios would not let their contract players appear on television. They viewed television as a deadly enemy, and fought it for years. Tyrone Power, a Fox contract player, was one such star whose studio barred him from our show — although I did get to meet him when his wife, the actress Linda Christian, was a guest. We did have a few movie stars on *We, the People*, including Glenn Ford and Charles Boyer, and this

JS, Glen Ford and announcer Dan Seymour.

was usually possible only because their studio contracts did not prevent them from appearing on television.

During my years on *We, the People*, I collected an array of effusive thank-you notes from our famous guests.

The composer Richard Rodgers telegraphed: "If I did anything wrong, I'm sorry. If I did anything, right I'm surprised." Irving Berlin thanked me and complimented our staff. Our custom was to send famous guests a gift, and Berlin loved the clock we sent.

Famed theater director Margo Jones wrote "I think you are doing a grand job and I marvel at it." Mary Garden, a great opera star of the 20s, wrote that "it was my first and delightful experience in television." Actor Boris Karloff, famous for his monster movie roles, also recorded his television debut on *We, the People*: "As you know it was my first experience of television and I appreciated your help a great deal, and am so glad that the show turned out alright."

Admiral Richard Byrd, explorer of the North Pole, wrote from the Navy Department in Washington: "...I came away from New York with a tremendous admiration for the way you fellows do things. It's very easy to see why *We, the People* is such a very great success. It is due to brains,

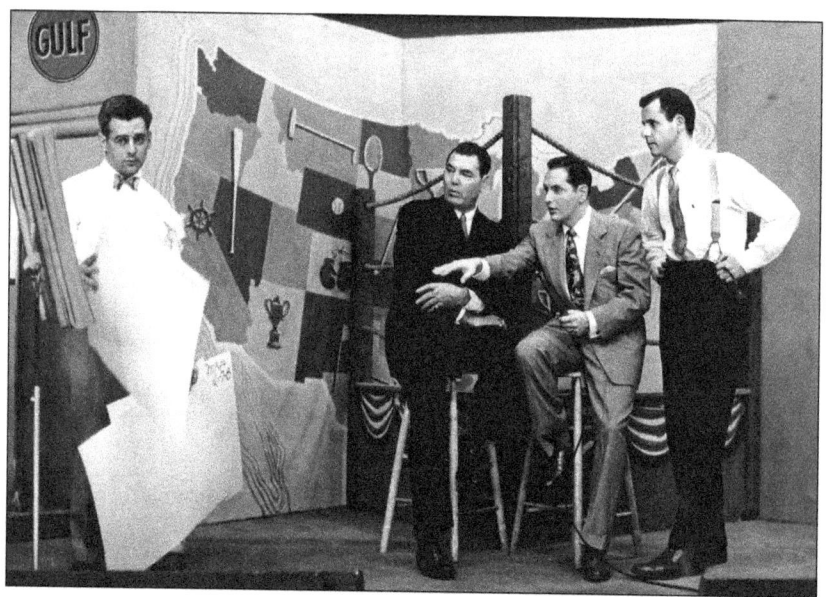

Heavyweight Champ Jack Dempsey rehearses cue cards.

plus a great capacity for pains."

Some time after Mary Martin, the star of the Broadway musical *South Pacific*, appeared on the show, a dear friend of mine who was suffering from terminal cancer told me that her one wish was to see *South Pacific*. The show was sold out, but I wrote to Martin and asked her for tickets for my friend, Jeannie. She sent them, and wrote me a letter thanking me for letting her do something for this lovely, very ill lady.

My favorite was perhaps the letter from Gloria Swanson, the great silent movie star from the early days of Hollywood. "Being a pioneer in the television business as well," Swanson wrote, "I should like you to know what a pleasure it was for me to be in your production of *We, the People*. It's the most technically advanced program I have ever been on and the best staff I have ever worked with."

At twenty-seven, I really enjoyed playing "daddy" to so many older people from all walks of life, people who were veterans in their own fields but who had never appeared on television before. I was in awe of them and, at the same time, they relied on me to make them look good in this new medium.

Not every guest on *We, the People* was as smooth as Boris Karloff or as gracious as Gloria Swanson. Like any live television crew, we sweated our way through our share of on-the-air crises.

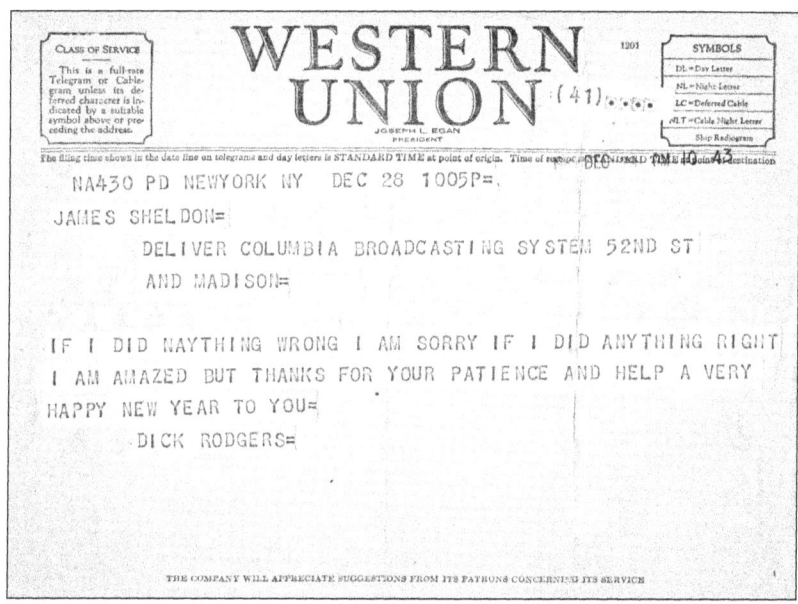

Richard Rodgers telegram.

Charles Laughton was one of the more difficult guests. He was not only a famous actor but also a director of theater and movies. At the time, Laughton was touring the country doing readings from the Bible, and *We, the People* invited him to deliver one of these performances on the air. Though he was as new to television as most of our other guests, Laughton did not take direction willingly. If I said, "Sit here," he would say, "I would rather stand." He read his piece well and the subsequent interview was good, but I had the feeling that Laughton didn't think much of television or of me.

My most nerve-wracking experience on *We, the People* occurred during the week in which Billie Holiday, the great blues singer, appeared as a guest. Holiday had a well-publicized substance abuse problem, and the story that she was to tell in her interview was that she had given up drugs and "straightened herself out." Unfortunately, that story was not entirely true.

We had a routine rehearsal schedule on the day of Billie's show. Each of the night's guests would be rehearsed separately, then the orchestra would rehearse the musical bridges and, for the musical guests, their songs. Then we would do a run-through of the entire program. We would then make whatever trims were necessary. At seven-thirty there would be a dress rehearsal and at nine o'clock, ready or not, we went on the air live for twenty-nine minutes and thirty seconds.

> SS
>
> BORIS KARLOFF
> BEVERLY HILLS, CALIFORNIA
> 12750 Mulholland Drive.
>
> Aug 10/48
>
> Dear Mr. Sheldon,
>
> Mr. Toby Rowland has forwarded your very nice letter to me here and I want to thank you very much indeed for your good wishes. As you know it was my first experience of television and I appreciated your help a great deal and am so glad that the show turned alright.
>
> Sincerely,
>
> Boris Karloff

Letters from Boris Karloff *(left)* and Gloria Swanson *(right)*.

Because she was performing that evening at the Apollo Theatre, Billie Holiday was excused from the dress rehearsal. Before that, though, we had the usual run-through in the afternoon with Billie, who walked through her interview with the emcee and then sang with the orchestra. "Lover Man." Beautiful.

Like all of the interviews on *We, the People*, Billie's chat with the emcee would appear spontaneous, but actually it was scripted. In radio, the performers had simply read from their scripts, but in television we relied on

THE PLAZA
FIFTH AVENUE AT 59TH STREET
NEW YORK

October 7, 1949

Mr. James Sheldon
Producer, WE THE PEOPLE
c/o Young & Rubicam
285 Madison Avenue
New York, N.Y.

Dear Mr. Sheldon:

Being a pioneer in the television business as well, I should like you to know what a pleasure it was for me to be in your production of WE, THE PEOPLE. It's the most technically advanced program I have ever been on, and the best staff I have ever worked with.

Lots of personal good wishes to you and continued success.

Sincerely yours,

[signature]

the then-new (but now common) system of printing the lines on cue cards that were held out of camera range. The guests could read their lines but still appeared to be chatting casually with the emcee. The only hitch was that, if an interview ran long during the dress, we had only a brief time to revise the cue cards with any deletions we made.

Dress rehearsal on the night of Billie's appearance showed us that we were over our mandatory twenty-nine minutes and thirty seconds of

JS with Governor Harold Stassen.

air-time. We had to make some cuts in each guest's interview. I met Billie in her dressing room and went over the cuts we planned to make to her segment. Billie replied that she would not go on unless her appearance was done the way she rehearsed it. She seemed out of it, and I could not reason with her. Reluctantly, I said we would put the cuts back.

A frantic rush of ideas swirled around in my head as I headed back to confer with Rod Erickson in the control room. We'll get back the original cue cards, I thought, and we'll try to cut somewhere else. I would just have to hope that somehow we would find a place to speed the show up. We had to get all the commercials in, or the sponsors would be out for blood.

As I reached the control room in the back of the theater, the stage manager on his headset notified us that Billie had walked out of the theater. All my plans to improvise had suddenly become moot, now that our big guest had pulled a disappearing act. Rod ran out of the control room. I had never been in a position like that ten minutes before airtime.

On stage, three small sets had been set up for the first two interviews and the first commercial. Calmly, like it was a routine I was used to, I told the stage manager to instruct the emcee, Dwight Wiest, to stretch the first act. This opening bit was an ad lib interview with a man who couldn't read music, but who played the musical saw.

"Put the commercial on second where Billie was supposed to be," I said, "and if she comes back we'll put her on next to closing."

I never asked Rod what he said to Billie, but whatever it was, it worked. She came back to the theater during the musical saw act and we prepared to go live with her song in the penultimate slot.

Meanwhile, the musical saw man had talked and talked but, desperate to stretch things as much as I could, I had not yet cued his performance. When I learned that Billie was back I had to stop stretching and start speeding up, so I sent a signal to Dwight via the stage manager. Dwight got the cue to wrap up the interview and the musical saw man in turn began to play his saw. As soon as the man started playing, I cued the audience applause and we went into the live commercial for Gulf Oil. The poor musical saw man never knew what hit him.

I thought it was terrible programming having two entertainment figures back to back, but Billie's fit of temper had left us no choice. The closer on that program had always been Charles Boyer, who was a wonderful actor and still a major motion picture star. That night, he was to recite a piece celebrating a current French holiday.

Once we finally got Billie on the air, she did her interview and then sang — not as beautifully as she had that afternoon but well enough. But

I was still running much too long, and I was afraid I'd be fired because we would go so far overtime that we wouldn't get to the final commercial.

It was Boyer who saved the day for me. Having seen what was happening with Billie, Boyer, instead of sticking to the script, kept his eye on the clock and trimmed his script perfectly, ad-libbing just the right number of cuts to get us into the commercial on time. I got off the air on

Cue card artists backstage.

time, and nobody was aware of any problems except for those of us who had witnessed them in the studio.

Boyer later confided in me, after I thanked him profusely, that he felt he had to do something because he had never seen such "unprofessional behavior" as that exhibited by Billie Holiday that night. And yet, no one ratted on Billie to the press. Everyone loved her in spite of her problems.

"The problems caused by video dual programs have been overcome," Josef Kaselow wrote in the New York *Herald-Tribune* as early as October 17, 1948. In that article, Kaselow quoted me as saying that *We, the People* had as many listeners as at any time in its fourteen year history, and that its television audience was one of the largest. Things that were effective on radio were even more so on television. Mrs. Spencer Tracy brought tears to radio listeners talking of her deaf son, but was even more moving when you could see her. The radio comic Mischa Auer was even funnier on the tube.

Though it is not widely remembered today, *We, the People* was a sizeable hit in 1948. Milton Berle, on the *Texaco Star Theatre*, and Ed Sullivan, with *Toast of the Town*, both made their television debuts weeks after *We, the People*; and yet those soon-to-be-superstars reached a smaller audience at first than our little show did. By September 1948, our simulcast had a TV rating in the upper bracket (31.5) and an average radio rating of 6.5. Of the top-rated radio programs in that month, *We, the People* came in fourth, behind only Walter Winchell, the *Lux Radio Theater*, and *Arthur Godfrey's Talent Scouts*. As opposed to Texaco who only reached a television audience, our sponsor, Gulf Oil, was able to reach the audiences of both radio and television and it only cost them an additional fifteen percent.

I stayed with *We, the People* as its producer-director for over two years. During that time, television audiences grew into the millions, and in 1950 the show (which would remain on television for another two years) was still going strong. But I was growing restless. Working with the young actors in those little blackout sketches I created to stitch together the guests on *We, the People* had given me a new goal. I wanted to direct dramas. It was time for me to move on.

Richard Rodgers
488 MADISON AVENUE • NEW YORK 22, N. Y.
Telephone MUrray Hill 8-3640

November
1st
1950

Mr. James Sheldon,
Young and Rubicam, Inc.,
285 Madison Avenue,
New York 17, N. Y.

Dear Jim:

    Congratulations on your new program. I dare say the congratulations should be directed to the "Holiday Hotel" people for having the wisdom to choose you, but anyway I hope to see you in the near future.

            Yours sincerely,

            Dick.

RR L

Congratulatory Letter from Richard Rodgers.

CHAPTER 2

Holiday Hotel to *Mister Peepers*: More Sets In Use

This from composer Richard Rodgers, dated November 1st, 1950 was one of the many congratulations for my moving on from *We, the People*.

Still on staff at Young & Rubicam, I took over direction of an entirely for-television weekly half-hour musical comedy, entitled *Holiday Hotel*. It was produced by the well-known nightclub impresario Monte Proser of the popular Copacabana in New York. Movie star Don Ameche was the host of the fictional hotel. There was the excellent Bernie Green Orchestra, a chorus of eight singers, eight dancers and each week the storyline had a guest star. It was telecast live from ABC's large television studio on 67th Street on Manhattan's west side where ABC studios still stands today.

The alternate week sponsors were both Young & Rubicam clients — Packard Motor Car and Cluett-Peabody, manufacturers of Arrow shirts. The sets, quite elaborate for the time, were by the talented art director, James McNaughton. There was a choral director and a choreographer as well, and I was put in charge of the show.

Proser wasn't around much. The live show had begun with another director and another star, the delightful Edward Everett Horton. For whatever political reasons they changed the actor playing the hotel manager and the director.

Don Ameche had been a major Hollywood star at Twentieth Century Fox for many years, playing romantic leads opposite Betty Grable and Alice Faye and was directed by Ernst Lubitsch in *Heaven Can Wait* opposite Gene Tierney. He had started as a radio announcer in Chicago and had a rich voice and was perhaps best known as Alexander Graham Bell in the Fox biopic film of the telephone's inventor. For years people affectionately called their telephone an Ameche. Fighting the new medium, the studios still wouldn't permit any of their contract players to be on television, but Ameche's long-term contract had recently expired.

In addition to the package that the agency had bought, there was some extra money budgeted that they could add for guest stars. I found out somehow that the terrific guest dancers on the show, Harold Lang and Helen Gallagher, were only getting fifteen hundred dollars, not the five thousand the agency was putting up, and the rest was being pocketed by Proser. I felt the money should go to make a better show and I told my agency supervisor. Proser didn't like me much after that but Ameche did and I stayed on the show for a year.

We also had composer-lyricist Irvin Graham ("You Better Go Now," "I Believe") writing special musical material every week and the guest stars included such delightful performers as Kitty Carlisle and Mary Boland. Kitty had done two films with Bing Crosby and is perhaps best remembered for her role in the Marx Brothers' *A Night at the Opera*. Mary had been at MGM for many films and on Broadway in the Cole Porter / Moss Hart musical *Jubilee*, which introduced such great songs as "Just One of Those Things" and "Begin the Beguine."

The Packard commercials were done live in the same studio, with a Packard automobile shown at one end. One night, Mary Boland was playing the role of a chambermaid. We were live on the air. The first half of the show went well and the commercial, with a specially designed shot, made the car look even better by shooting from one end of the large studio to the other. Over this picture we superimposed the Packard name. Just as it hit the air, Mary Boland, in her chambermaid costume, unaware, walked across the stage dragging her large broom.

Agency personnel in the control room screamed "Get her out!" "No!" I said. I didn't want to upset her and possibly spoil her performance for the rest of the show. She continued across the stage dragging her large broom completely unaware of being on camera. The next day the client called me to tell me what a brilliant touch that was — tying the show together with the commercial.

Directing only for television, and not radio as well, allowed me to experiment with different camera moves and lenses. The facile crew was terrific in a large studio with no audience. We could try visual moves that were as imitative of Orson Welles' use of camera as this kind of show would allow. It was fun to do, but with a choreographer, a choral director and a bandleader, I didn't fully feel creatively in charge. I longed to do dramas.

After *Holiday Hotel* went off the air in 1951, I still worked at Young and Rubicam and as there were no shows available for me to direct, I was appointed to supervise commercials on other Y&R shows. This just meant that I visited the control room of each show to ensure that the commercial went on the air properly.

Around this time, I received a phone call from my friend, director Ralph Levy, the original camera director on *We, the People*, who was now at CBS in Los Angeles. Levy had a friend of a friend, a young actor, coming to New York, and would I help him get started? A few days later, a handsome twenty-one year-old named James Dean showed up in my office.

I happened to have on my desk some copies of an audition scene from the comedy-drama series *Mama*. The producer, Ralph Nelson, needed a replacement for the juvenile lead, Dick Van Patten, who was being drafted into the army. I gave Jimmy a copy of the scene to read for me. He did a good reading, good enough for me to call *Mama*'s casting director, Doris Quinlin, and recommend that she meet him. I told her that Dean reminded me of a young Brando. That was a compliment, given that Brando was then at the height of his stardom, but it was also specific to the show: Marlon had originated the same part on stage in John Van Druten's play, *I Remember Mama*, which had led to the hit film, radio, and now TV adaptations.

Jimmy read for them and got the part. I was a hero to everyone: Jimmy, Ralph Levy, the people at *Mama*. Then Van Patten was rejected by the army for health reasons, and kept his role on *Mama*. Jimmy rejoined the swollen ranks of unemployed, unknown young actors in New York.

Sometimes Jimmy would drop by my office, to chat or borrow a few bucks. I called some other directors I knew to try to find him work. I called my friend, the talent agent Jane Deacy. Jane had gotten her start as the switchboard operator at the large and powerful Louis Schurr Agency, and had just recently opened her own office. She and Jimmy hit it off, she got him into a Broadway production of a new play by N. Richard Nash called *See the Jaguar*. The play didn't do well, but Jimmy was very good in a flashy part and received good reviews. He and I kept up our friendship.

This supervisory job at Y & R also brought me to the control room of the *Philco/Goodyear Playhouse*, the prestigious dramatic show overseen by NBC staff producer Fred Coe. Jane Deacy had introduced me to Fred early in his TV career, when he produced a fifteen-minute musical series for one of her clients, Kyle MacDonnell. MacDonnell had been one of the first television stars in New York.

The *Philco/Goodyear Playhouse* was beginning to earn serious critical notice. Fred had two directors alternating weekly: Delbert Mann (who later won an Oscar for the film of *Marty*, which he had directed first on

Philco) and Gordon Duff. I was sitting in the control room supervising the Goodyear commercial when I overheard Fred talking about the thirteenth week with Delbert about whom they should get to direct.

I butted in with, "How about me?" I guess they were willing to give me a chance, and after all I was the agency representative, so the agency couldn't complain if it went wrong. I was a safe bet for Coe.

JS directing Jean Pierre Aumont.

This would be my big break. When I received the script, I saw that the show was a biographical piece about Louis Braille, the blind Frenchman who invented the Braille system which enables people to read by touch. Jean Pierre Aumont, a prominent French movie star who had begun an American career during the war, was set to play Braille.

At first, the Goodyear show went without a hitch. We had a reading of the script with the producer and writer present, and then several days of blocking and rehearsing with the cast. Then a run-through, with comments by the executives, and a day with the cameras, lining up the shots one by one. During our second day on camera, we did another run-through and a dress rehearsal. At the end of that long day, we went on the air LIVE.

After the dress rehearsal, we found that we were running longer than our allotted fifty-nine minutes and thirty seconds. Fred suggested a cut, and I agreed that it wouldn't hurt the story.

On the air that night, when we came to the scene following the one we had cut, I realized that I had made a mistake. I had told the cast and crew about the scene we were deleting, and how to transition into the next one. But I had forgotten about the camera cables. In 1952, television cameras required careful maneuvering because of their bulky electrical cables, which were plugged into the outlets in the studio walls. One of the tedious, nuts-and-bolts tasks every live director had to deal with was planning his camera moves in a way that kept the cables from getting tangled.

That night, Jean-Pierre was supposed to have a big close-up during the scene following the one we cut. But I had forgotten to correct for the camera positions that would have changed during the missing scene. The camera that was to get Jean-Pierre's close-up was supposed to move into place during the cut scene, but another camera's cable was in the way. So the scene had to play in a wide shot. Jean-Pierre played his big scene far back on the stage, with a potted palm in the foreground dominating the shot. The show went off on time.

Afterward, in the control room, I apologized profusely to everyone. Fred Coe then asked me "Don't you have any confidence in yourself?"

I quickly realized that no one had noticed the lack of that close-up except for Jean-Pierre and myself. Fred taught me a valuable lesson that night. In the future, whenever an error was made, I never went out of my way to bring it to anyone's attention.

It was in that same NBC control room, earlier in that same day, that Fred brought up an idea which led to my next directing job. He mentioned that he had just seen a young comic actor, Wally Cox, who was appearing nightly at the Village Vanguard club in Greenwich Village. I had seen Cox too, and I told Fred how much I liked his off-kilter sense of humor. Fred replied that he was thinking of doing a series built around Cox. And he asked: would I like to direct it?

Even though it meant I had to leave Young & Rubicam, joining the show that would be called *Mister Peepers* was a good move. About that time, advertising executive Nat Wolf had joined the agency and pointed out that it was more profitable for them to hire a director when needed (and bill the client plus the 15% commission) than to keep directors on staff at the agency's expense. The handwriting was on the wall. I became a freelance director at just the right time.

Wally Cox as Mister Peepers.

I was doubly fortunate for I was continuing to work for one of the great men in television. Fred Coe was one of the first important producers and innovators. He had a temper which was well-known, but he always treated me as a collaborator. He had a tendency to scream "I wanna see the Vice-President in charge of properties!" if he didn't like a prop someone was given. He had the studio hopping, but all he really cared about was the quality of the show we were working on. What made it tricky is he was having a romance with his secretary despite having a wife and kids. I was privy to the information but didn't talk about it. Eventually he left his first wife and married that secretary, but kept the temper for when he wasn't getting what he wanted from NBC.

We did the *Peepers* pilot, live, only a few weeks before the show debuted. The Ford Motor Company saw the pilot and bought *Mister Peepers* as a summer replacement for the Ford Theater, to begin in July. I directed the half-hour show each week in the Center Theater in Rockefeller Center — a larger space than we needed, but it had the pivotal advantage of being vacant — and *Mister Peepers* was on the air.

Robinson Peepers was a shy, quiet, slow-moving science teacher whose efforts to do the right thing always seemed to backfire, but who prevailed at the end of every episode. David Swift created the character, and Jim Fritzell was the main writer at first. (Later Fritzell teamed with Everett Greenbaum, another funny comic writer). *Mister Peepers* was a realistic show with magical overtones tailored to Wally's particular brand of gentle humor. People often ask if Wally was like his eccentric TV persona in real life. He may have exaggerated it slightly, but he really was a person from another world. On *Mister Peepers*, I rarely gave him any direction apart from technical instructions, on where to move or pick up the pace a bit. The character, derived from his nightclub act, was already set when we started the show.

The rest of the regular cast comprised Mr. Peepers' fellow teachers. Joe Foley played the principal, Mr. Gurney, and the wonderfully multidimensional Marion Lorne appeared as his wife. Patricia Benoit played the school nurse, who was also the romantic interest for Mr. Peepers. It was a sweet show in which the odd science teacher's out-of-kilter relationship with the world around him led to lots of physical gags: a bubbling water fountain that always hit him in the face, or a typewriter carriage that wouldn't stay attached. Peepers was the underdog who somehow always came out on top.

We started rehearsals for *Mister Peepers* each Monday and went on the air live on Fridays. Compared to an hour-long dramatic program, it was an easy schedule, although there were unusual special effects that had to be set up and tested, like the flying cartridge off Mr. Peepers' typewriter or the open window that kept falling closed on cue. And like on all comedy shows there were also frequent rewrites trying to make it funnier.

David Swift, who I had met when he wrote an episode of *Holiday Hotel*, was around most of the time on *Mister Peepers*. In the early rehearsals for *Mister Peepers*, Marion had trouble remembering her lines. Because she wasn't saying David's words the way he wrote them, he wanted to replace her. Wally and I nevertheless found her delightful and we convinced David and Fred Coe that she would be letter-perfect by the time we went on the air. David relented. Marion never did deliver his dialogue exactly the way he wrote it but, necessity being the mother of invention, she created a wonderful character that never seemed sure of what to say. Her dithering became the source of the humor and, indeed, the basis of a whole new career for Marion in her mature years. Later she used basically the same routine when she was on Elizabeth Montgomery's long-running sitcom *Bewitched*.

I have to take credit for one other crucial piece of casting on *Mister Peepers*. In that summer of 1952, my wife and I rented a beach cottage on Fire Island. Wally came to visit one weekend and, just as Mister Peepers might have done, he spent some time wandering the lonely beach, poking the eyes out of dead seagulls on the sand with a stick.

One of my neighbors, across the dune in Fair Harbor, was a woman named Florence Randall, who was a friend of my cousin Gertrude's. Gertrude kept after me to give her friend's husband a job. The weekend after Wally's visit, I was lying on the beach preparing the next week's script for *Mister Peepers*. I looked up and noticed a young man doing the same thing Wally had done: poking at the corpses of seagulls with a stick. The fellow turned out to be Florence's husband — Tony Randall — and I thought that he and Wally might get along. There was a one-page scene in that episode which introduced the history teacher at Mr. Peepers' school. I called Fred Coe and asked if I could use Tony. Fred okayed the casting, and on Monday morning Tony was with us for the start of rehearsals. The chemistry between him and Wally was so instantaneous at the first read-through that, by Friday, the one-page scene had expanded to five. Tony stayed on the show for several years and garnered enough attention that he starred in several feature film comedies after *Mister Peepers* went off the air. Later, after he was a movie star, Tony would always introduce me as the director who gave him his big break. Even after he died, his second wife, Heather (whom he had married after Florence died following nearly fifty years of marriage) introduced me to their son, Jefferson, as the man who gave Dad his big break. Not many actors that I was to work with were as appreciative.

Mister Peepers was well received. "In a dull season of summer TV replacements," *Time* wrote, "one show last week was giving television a pleasant ringing in the funny bone." The same review went on: "Shrewdly and precisely tied together are the work of writer David Swift and director James Sheldon. But it is 27 year-old Wally Cox who gives the show the real flavor."

Peepers went off after the contracted summer run, with no guarantee that it would come back, despite the good notices. Wally Cox's agent, Gloria Safier, called to thank me for helping her client and asked if she could do anything for me. I said, "Find me a job."

"Where do you want to work?" she asked. "CBS," I said. At the time, they had some of the best dramatic shows on television.

Gloria was a marvelous agent. The next week, she had me working at CBS. It was the career move I had been eager to make, although at first I had a pang of regret, because *Mister Peepers* was picked up and returned to NBC's lineup (replacing a new comedy, *Doc Corkle*, that quickly flopped) right after I started at CBS. *Peepers*, now directed by the capable and tragically short-lived Hal Keith, ran for three more seasons and remained a critic's darling. It is one of the few live situation comedies that retains a cult following and, more than fifty years later, kinescopes of the early episodes were released in two large DVD sets.

In live television, years before there were home recording devices, I never got to watch my shows; when directing a live show, I was so busy calling shots that I couldn't really *see* the show. With the *Mister Peepers* DVDs, I got to really watch the show for the first time, and it felt great to finally be able to enjoy the clever writing and Wally's weird sense of humor for myself. Marlon Brando, who grew up with Wally and roomed with him in New York, wrote in his autobiography that Wally Cox was the only true genius he knew.

CHAPTER 3

Studio One and *Robert Montgomery Presents:* The Golden Age of Television

Mister Peepers had been not only a success and a joy to work on, but also the first TV show in which I had really felt like a vital creative contributor. Though I only directed fewer than thirteen episodes, I had selected the composer, Bernard Green (from *Holiday Hotel*) and some key cast members, and I had helped to set the tone of the show's unique humor. Now, at CBS, I hoped to do the same thing on some weightier shows. But first I ran afoul of the kind of politicking that people often associate with the television industry.

On the strength of my success with *Mister Peepers*, William Dozier, the head of production at CBS, wanted to assign me to help craft another new comedy show, this one a vehicle for the comedian Red Buttons. But Red's agent at William Morris sabotaged my chance at the job. The agent, George Gruskin, fabricated a whole story about how I really hadn't directed *Peepers*, and how I didn't actually know anything about comedy. That lie, I learned years later, was a ploy of Gruskin's to secure the directing job for another client of his.

The next time I crossed paths with Gruskin, the tables were turned. He was trying to sell me one of his clients, and I reminded him of the Red Buttons incident. Gruskin apologized, offering the excuse that his job was to sell his clients in any way he could. It was an unpleasant experience all around and, sadly, I heard later that Gruskin lost his wits and had to be institutionalized.

Coincidentally, I had worked with Gruskin's wife, the comic actress Florence Halop, not long before my run-in with him. She had a one-of-a-kind, gravelly voice that made her ideal to play the switchboard operator at *Holiday Hotel*. Florence, I liked; her husband, not so much.

I had been hired at CBS as a contract director, which meant that I could be assigned to any show at the network. My first job at CBS proved to be a real comedown from *Mister Peepers*. It was a daytime game show, *There's One in Every Family*, hosted by John Reid King.

I wasn't happy directing quiz shows, but fortunately I was soon transferred to a more agreeable series, movie star Eddie Albert's afternoon talk show. I had been a fan of his since I was sixteen and saw him in *Brother Rat* on Broadway, and later in the Warner Bros. film version. In 1939 I

JS with Red Buttons and Tallulah Bankhead

had sneaked backstage at the Alvin Theater (now the Neil Simon Theater) to get his autograph after I saw the Rodgers & Hart musical he was starring in, *The Boys From Syracuse*. Now Albert was the headliner in a pleasant half-hour chat/musicale, and I was to be his director. *The Eddie Albert Show* ran on CBS five times a week, during which Albert would talk to his audience and sing some songs with the Norman Paris Trio. A female singer accompanied him for some numbers; at first it was the delicious Anita Ellis (who had been Rita Hayworth's voice double in the movies) and after her the lovely Ellen Hanley. I directed the show for eleven weeks. It was a daytime show, not prime-time, and still a step backward from drama, but nevertheless I enjoyed it.

One day in April 1953, I was in the control room calling shots for *The Eddie Albert Show* when my assistant director, Tony Barr, contradicted my camera call. (Tony later became a vice president at ABC, and recommended me for many shows.) Lights went on in the darkened control room, and there I was on the screen. Tony had ordered one of the cameras to turn one hundred and eighty degrees and aim right at me. Eddie told the audience I had just become a father, and then sang the wonderful "Soliloquy" from Rodgers and Hammerstein's *Carousel*. Unfortunately, there was no kinescope made of that show, and I never got to have a copy to show my first son, James, Jr., what I was doing on the day he was born.

In the summer of 1953, I finally moved up to direct one of the top evening dramatic anthologies. *Studio One* was CBS's answer to NBC's *Philco/Goodyear Playhouse*, which had set the early standard for quality television drama. *Studio One* didn't have the stable of young playwrights that Fred Coe had on *Philco*, but instead staged adaptations of famous books. During most of the year, two veteran live directors, Franklin Schaffner and Paul Nickell, alternated in the control room of *Studio One*. But during the summer, those two went on vacation, as did the producer, Felix Jackson. The name of the show changed to the *Studio One Summer Theater*. John Haggott took over as producer in the interim, and CBS tried out some substitute directors, including me.

On *Studio One*, I was delighted to be directing a different group of good actors every week. I directed Kevin McCarthy and Constance Ford in a Raymond Chandler story, "The King in Yellow." Another Studio One I remember fondly was an adaptation of Rudyard Kipling's *The Light That Failed*. It was an old-fashioned story about a painter losing his sight, but it was Kipling. Ronald Colman had starred in a very successful film version. John Haggott and I lined up a good British cast, including Melville Cooper (who had been in the first Broadway play I had ever seen) and the great star of the D'Oyly Carte Gilbert and Sullivan company, Martyn Green.

I had received a call from a young agent, George Morris, who worked for Jane Broder, a well-known talent agent. He knew his clients and I had confidence in his opinions. George suggested a young Canadian actor for the lead, and Christopher Plummer made his American debut and did very well. A brilliant career followed, and our paths have crossed over the years.

On this show, we started rehearsals on Monday and on that Friday the sponsor, Westinghouse, decided the title had to be changed. Westinghouse was a power company, and couldn't associate itself with any light that failed. "The Gathering Night" emerged as the new title, and although my mostly British cast was irate about this indignity we were committing against Kipling, the client had the final say.

The last of my *Studio One Summer Theater*s was "The Shadow of a Man," featuring Douglas Dick, out from Hollywood, and another erst-

JS and cast of *The Gathering Night*.

while French star, Claude Dauphin. But my champion at the network, Bill Dozier had been transferred to CBS's gigantic new Television City facility, which had just opened in Los Angeles. I wasn't sure what the new powers that be would assign me to direct for the fall of 1953, but continuing with *Studio One* seemed unlikely.

A year earlier, in between the *Mister Peepers* pilot and when the show went on the air, I had been hired to direct one episode of the dramatic series *Robert Montgomery Presents*. Montgomery had been a major movie star in Hollywood *(Here Comes Mr. Jordan, Night Must Fall)* during the 1930s and '40s, and now he was the host and occasional star of this live television anthology. Montgomery's business partner, an independent talent agent named John Gibbs, hired me to direct an episode guest-starring

James Daly and Barbara Britton. The Montgomery show took an unusual approach to casting, in that the supporting parts in the summer shows were filled each week by a sort of stock company. It included Margaret Hayes, John Newland (later a major TV director himself), and the teen-aged Elizabeth Montgomery, who was just beginning her career on her father's program. Once the stock company had been put to use, we then hired outside actors for any remaining parts. I cast Ed Hastings, a recent Yale Drama School graduate, as a bellboy.

"Do you have a part for my roommate?" Ed asked me. Everything had been cast except for a one-line bit, a guy sitting around the hotel swimming pool (which, incidentally, was painted on the studio floor). Ed said that would be great, and his roommate played the part. It was Paul Newman!

In his one scene, I had Paul sitting beside the painted-on swimming pool in his bathing trunks. Unbeknownst to me, the line producer came by and said to the wardrobe lady, "His legs are too skinny. Give him a robe." Paul had to wear the robe during the show. It's hard to imagine any producer making the same call a few years later, after Newman became a major star.

Robert Montgomery Presents was telecast from NBC's Studio 8H in Radio City, which is the same studio to which I had been assigned on my first day as a page boy eleven years before. Toscanini rehearsed the wonderful NBC Symphony in 8H that day. I felt at home there.

That feeling came back to me a year later, when John Gibbs called to offer me a regular job directing *Robert Montgomery Presents*. The catch: I had to sign with Gibbs as my agent. I didn't like the blackmail, but my future at CBS looked uncertain, and my current agent, Gloria Safier, said she would release me from our contract. I left the CBS staff in the fall of 1953 and began work, as a freelancer, on every third *Montgomery* show.

In the brief window before my first fall show for them, I was hired by John Haggott, who had also moved on from CBS, to direct an episode of the *Theatre Guild On The Air*. The Guild, headed by Lawrence Langner and Armina Marshall, was a prominent Broadway production outfit that launched its own dramatic anthology that year; the sponsor was United States Steel, and the show was also known as the *U.S. Steel Hour*.

My episode starred Jessie Royce Landis (later a memorable scene-stealer in Hitchcock's *To Catch a Thief* and *North by Northwest*). It was an hour-long original drama by William Kendall Clarke, with a supporting cast that included Walter Matthau, Barbara Baxley, and a twenty-one year-old Anthony Perkins. Walter had played a bit part for me in the

Mister Peepers pilot, and our paths would cross again. Tony and Walter played baseball outside the rehearsal hall whenever we rehearsed scenes they were not in. As for Jessie Royce Landis, I was thrilled to work with her. Once, years earlier, I had flirted with being an actor, and had auditioned to replace a cast member in *Kiss and Tell*, in which Jessie was starring on Broadway. Unfortunately, it was not to be. After I made it through two callbacks, the director George Abbott showed up to make the decision. Abbott was my idol, and I froze! My knees literally shook.

Studio One had been a CBS show, and the *U. S. Steel Hour* was on ABC. *Robert Montgomery Presents*, which would be my new home for a while, was broadcast by NBC. Those network affiliations made little difference to the audience, but for a television director they were of great importance. The reason is that the cameramen at each network belonged to different unions, and each union had negotiated a different set of rules with its respective network.

At CBS, a director could talk directly to the cameramen. But at NBC, a director was not supposed to interact with the cameramen. Instead, he or she had to talk to the technical director, who then relayed those instructions to the cameramen. The technical director was the guy who took the director's cue as to when to change the camera shot, and who lined up the shots with the director on the floor. A good director had to learn how to handle both systems, although most of us preferred the simplicity of the CBS setup. At NBC, I found a simple way of skirting the extraneous step. If I talked loudly when I addressed the technical director, the cameramen could overhear me and begin to implement my directions before the TD repeated them. It was a bit silly, but I got used to it.

My first show for *Robert Montgomery Presents*, "Harvest," starred Dorothy Gish, the famous silent screen star. It was their Thanksgiving show, a story about a farm boy who wants to go to the big city, and I was able to cast my friend James Dean in that role. Ed Begley played Jimmy's father, and the character actor Vaughn Taylor appeared as his aged grandfather. Taylor was only in his forties, younger than Ed Begley, but as the pressures of live television were too much for many elderly actors, he had developed a lucrative specialty of playing senior citizens.

In those days, music in live television was selected by the director in advance and cleared by the network's music department for broadcast. Pre-recorded cues were selected by the director during the rehearsal period, then during the telecast the music played on a turntable in the control room. For "Harvest," being the Thanksgiving show, I picked very emotional music, like Nelson Eddy's recording of the Lord's Prayer.

The rehearsal schedule for *Robert Montgomery Presents* was not that different from the other live hour-long dramas I had done. We read through the script on Monday, started the actors' blocking on Tuesday, and then rehearsed on Wednesday and Thursday. Mr. Montgomery always wanted a run through on Friday so he could go away for the weekend. That meant that we were rushing to get a performance for an hour show ready in four days. It was a tough schedule. Another of the directors on *Montgomery* came up with a famous line: he said, "Do you want it good? Or do you want it Monday?" Montgomery wanted both! Saturday was our day off, right in the middle of an episode's preparation, and then we reassembled on Sunday to line up each shot with the camera crew. We'd run a scene and then walk through it, piece by piece, with the actors. The camera crew would make notes on their movements. Usually, I streamlined this process by giving the technical director and the sound mixer a script marked with the specific shots I wanted from each camera. Monday was our broadcast day. We finished blocking on camera in the morning, then did a run-through and a dress rehearsal. Then, ready or not, we went on the air at nine-thirty. It was a fast week.

Arthur Franz and I had been pageboys together at NBC radio, and since then he had become a successful actor on Broadway and in films. He and June Lockhart starred in my next *Robert Montgomery*, "The Steady Man," which was telecast during the first week of 1954. A day or so before we were to be on the air, President Eisenhower decided to make a televised speech, which forced NBC to cut our show by fifteen minutes. We scrambled to shorten the script and came up with a version that we liked. In fact, Arthur's wife, the actress and later talent agent Adele Longmire, told me it was one of his best performances. When I moved to Hollywood the following year, Arthur and Adele became good friends.

Later that month, I started rehearsals for "The 17th of June," a very interesting script based on a series of *New Yorker* magazine articles on the uprisings in East Berlin. Film star Wendell Corey was set to do the lead by his agents at MCA. He arrived for the first reading accompanied by Ina Bernstein from the agency. Ina was a novice, and Corey hated the script and was angry at MCA for booking him to do it. I had to serve as mediator, and Ina was forever grateful that I managed to convince Corey that the script was really much better than he thought. A week later, he came off splendidly in the show. In 1958, after I had moved to the west coast, I directed every other episode of a filmed series called *Harbor Command* with Corey in San Francisco. He was a fine actor, but had a well-known drinking problem. To keep us on schedule, I spent many late nights keeping him happy in San Francisco. By keeping him company, I prevented Corey from getting lonely and he drank less.

My fourth show for *Montgomery* starred the great stage actor Walter Hampden. It was a story about aging called "Such a Busy Day Tomorrow." Most actors learned the script during rehearsals, but Hampden showed up on the first day with his lines fully memorized. I guess that, as an elderly actor with only a week to prepare, he found that to be a safer way to work. In any case, he was excellent.

Then I did a story called "My Little Girl," with the screen star James Dunn. He and actress Sally Eilers were a romantic team in several films in the thirties. He was very easy to work with and Lee Remick, in one of her first roles, played his daughter.

This episode's title reminded me of Rodger and Hammerstein's brilliant song "Soliloquy" from *Carousel* (the song Eddie Albert sang to me when I became a father). In that song the leading man learns he's going to be a dad and dreams of his little girl. I thought it would be a great way to back the opening titles.

One of the employee's within NBC's music clearance department insisted I could not use Rodgers and Hammerstein without permission and she haughtily implied it was going to be an impossibility to secure. In her presence I telephoned Dick Rodgers and explained the problem.

"Oscar," he shouted, "Jimmy Sheldon wants to use the 'Soliloquy' on *Robert Montgomery*, ok?" A moment later he came back with "Ok, Jim, have NBC send us a memo."

The music clearance lady was impressed and I was pleased.

We couldn't afford a singer but they allowed me a trumpet player and I had him play the haunting melody in silhouette with the titles supered over. It set a great mood whether you were familiar with the tune or not. Lee went on to great stardom but Dunn never did much in films after his brilliant performance in *A Tree Grows in Brooklyn*.

A year later, I directed another *Robert Montgomery* with Lee, and I used her own mother, Pat Remick, to play her character's mother in the show. I had first worked with Lee when she was only sixteen, and we kept up our friendship. Later she married another television director, Bill Colleran, and invited me to the wedding.

As fulfilling as it was to finally be directing a dramatic hour every few weeks, I was always looking for ways to expand my creative horizons. One way I did that was by dabbling in writing. For the Montgomery show, I adapted a book called *End of a Mission* into a teleplay, which I directed with young Leslie Nielsen. I enjoyed my added involvement in that segment, but I think I only got an extra forty dollars for my script. This was before I joined the union.

Around the same time, I started to direct other shows, alternating with my *Montgomery* show every third week. NBC hired me to direct for a half-hour drama called *Armstrong Circle Theater*, which was considered by many to be one of the best anthology series during the "Golden Age"

Jackie Cooper and JS, with wife and son in frame.

of television. *Armstrong* featured original scripts by noted writers, and its sponsors' guidelines specifically called for the avoidance of violence in the stories. The producer, Hudson Faussett, was a charming man to work for, and at the time he was going out with Lee Remick's mother.

My first *Armstrong* show starred Madge Evans, the former movie star, and Robert Keith, a prominent Broadway actor whose son Brian was just getting started in the movies. It went well, and the next one, "Two People," with William Prince and Louisa Horton, received a very favorable review in *The New Yorker*. My direction was singled out for praise. Things were going well for me.

James Dean and I worked together again on another *Armstrong*, "The Bells of Cockaigne," featuring Gene Lockhart in the lead role. It was a sentimental half-hour about a widower whose dream is to visit his birthplace in Ireland. But when he wins a lottery, instead of making the trip, he decides to give the money to a young man (Dean) with a gambling habit who is trying to reform now that he has a baby on the way.

It had only been a short time since we worked together on "Harvest," but Jimmy had changed.

With Jane Deacy's help, he had gotten noticed on Broadway, and Warner Bros. had just cast him in Elia Kazan's upcoming film of Steinbeck's *East of Eden*. Jimmy had been nothing but cooperative on "Harvest," but during "The Bells of Cockaigne," he was late for dress rehearsal. I gave him a talking to. Gene had told me confidentially that Jimmy kept changing his lines and staging, and without mentioning Gene's name, I told Jimmy that the other actors were having difficulty working with him.

Jimmy replied, with complete sincerity, that the actors loved him. Why, Gene Lockhart loved him! I think Jimmy was just unaware of other people's worlds. He was doing his thing, his way, and it worked well for him, but it often left the other actors without anything to play off of.

Despite our difficulties on "The Bells of Cockaigne," Jimmy and I maintained our friendship when I later moved to Hollywood. Two weeks before he was killed, we went to a rehearsal at NBC in Burbank of a live television adaptation of *Our Town* which was starring Frank Sinatra, Eva Marie Saint and Paul Newman with songs by Jimmy McHugh. This type of special was a once-a-month show that Fred Coe produced. The next month, Jimmy was to star in an adaptation of Ernest Hemingway's *The Battler*. Jimmy wanted to see the studio set up and we enjoyed sitting through the *Our Town* dress rehearsal. Jimmy died before he could do his episode. Since time was short, Fred cast Paul Newman in Jimmy's role. It was a turning point in Paul's career. His one film had been a flop, but he was so good in the role of the prizefighter, he became a big star.

I was with Jimmy the Sunday before he was killed in that terrible, famous car accident. The last time I saw him, he told me about how he had gotten a new Porsche, but that George Stevens, the director of his current film, *Giant*, wouldn't let him drive it until he was finished with principal photography. The first day Jimmy drove the car, he was killed. It was only afterward that *Rebel Without a Cause* and *Giant* were released and solidified Jimmy's status as an icon. I couldn't bear to see *Giant* when it was first released. When I finally did watch the film, twenty-five years later, it was with Jim's co-star Rock Hudson in his private screening room.

CHAPTER 4

Bus Stop:
Learning From the Master

During the early fifties, I was hitting my stride as a live TV director, but I still harbored notions of moving into the theater. It was my first love. The forties and fifties were a golden era in the theater, and as a New Yorker I took full advantage of that. When I wasn't working on a television segment, I was often attending theater. In New York, I caught every Ethel Merman musical and every Helen Hayes play. I saw the Lunts do wonderful dramas by wonderful playwrights, and sometimes less than memorable plays that they made worthwhile with their incredible charisma. Katherine Cornell, Ruth Gordon, and the greatest of them all, Laurette Taylor, played on Broadway in these years, and I was fortunate enough to see them all. The performance I remember most vividly was Laurette Taylor's in *The Glass Menagerie*. I first saw the new Tennessee Williams play in Chicago, before it opened in New York. I was supervising a radio show that originated there, and had to go to Chicago on weekends, which is how I got the early preview of that historic moment in American theater.

Through my friendship with his wife, the actress and teacher, Stella Adler, I had gotten to know Harold Clurman. He was one of the top three directors in the theater then, along with Elia Kazan and George Abbott. I felt I had to take advantage of my connection to Clurman to further my education in the arts. I was working steadily as a freelance director in television, but I felt there was still much to learn about directing, and the theater seemed like the place to do it. I asked Harold if I could assist him on his next project, and stay close to him to observe how he worked.

Harold said he never had assistants. I replied that I would be giving up a thousand dollars a week to do this, but that it was worth it because I wanted to learn from him. I think Harold was impressed with my earning power and he consented. His new play was to be another of the classic Broadway shows of that era: *Bus Stop*, by William Inge. For six weeks I was at every rehearsal of this terrific play, watching a marvelous cast headed by Kim Stanley, the legendary actress who created the part later played by Marilyn Monroe in the film version. Elaine Stritch and Anthony Ross were there too, and Jerome Courtland had been cast as the male lead, cowboy Beau Decker. Unfortunately, just before the play opened, he was let go and Albert Salmi replaced him. The producers had wanted Salmi originally, but he was tied up in the play *The Rainmaker*. When it closed suddenly, Salmi became available. After Courtland got mediocre reviews in *Bus Stop*'s Philadelphia tryout, the powers that be decided to go for Salmi. The chemistry between him and Kim was perfect.

Jerry Courtland wasn't a method actor, like Kim Stanley; he was more of a Hollywood personality and Disney-type leading man. He went home, and the play opened to rave reviews. Jerry and I worked together later on *West Point Story*, and after he began producing at Disney we crossed paths many times.

I leaned a lot watching the mounting of *Bus Stop*, particularly during the first week, when Clurman broke down the script. I also learned that I already knew a lot! It was a relief to find, after watching Clurman working with his cast, that the methods I had developed on my own were pretty sound. I came away from *Bus Stop* with added confidence in my own technique as a director.

Having had a wonderful time being a small part of Broadway in its golden era, I went back to my day job, directing *Robert Montgomery Presents* and *Armstrong Circle Theater*. In the fall of 1954, I added a third series to my regular rotation. *Modern Romances* was a daytime serial with a different story each week, hosted by Martha Scott, who had created the lead in *Our Town* on Broadway. The scripts were a bit turgid; they often felt as if they had originated as hour-long scripts and then been padded out to stretch over five half-hours. I started *Modern Romances* with the agreement that whenever I was doing another show, my assistant, Tom Reynolds would take over as director.

The three shows I was directing at the end of 1954 were popular (all of them would stay on the air for another three seasons, or longer), and conceivably I could have stayed with them for quite a while. But two new offers came along, right at the same time, and suddenly live television sounded less exciting than some of the other possibilities that were available to me.

One was in the theater. Arthur Laurents, an up-and-coming playwright, liked my work on television and knew that I had worked with

Clurman. He was beginning work on a new musical, which would have a book by Laurents and choreography by the genius Jerome Robbins. Robbins would also be directing, but Arthur had concerns about his ability to guide the actors' performances. He asked me if I would co-direct with Robbins — Jerry would stage the dances, and I would be responsible for staging the book. I was very interested, but there were drawbacks. The salary offer was only $200 a week, and since Robbins was a known quantity and I was not, my credit would be not as the book director but as his assistant.

The other offer came via a phone call from my old boss, Bill Dozier, who was now running CBS's Television City studios in Hollywood. Would I come west to rejoin the CBS staff, this time in Hollywood, and direct the new situation comedy *Professional Father*? Dozier would pay me $850 a week, along with all expenses of moving my family and myself to Los Angeles.

It would have been a much more difficult decision had I somehow known that the Laurents/Robbins musical was going to turn into *West Side Story*. But at the time, the CBS offer held more promise, and my wife and I decided to pack up and head west. The producers of *Robert Montgomery Presents* and *The Armstrong Circle Theater* were very cooperative in releasing me from my commitments but Stark-Layton, the producers of the *Modern Romances*, insisted that I buy out my contract before they would let me go. Grudgingly, I did so.

I had been to California only twice before: once in 1944, when I had the offer of an acting contract from MGM, and again in 1946 when I went to visit my dear friend, the actress Geraldine Brooks, who was making a picture at Warner Bros. This time, I was off to Hollywood as a director with a guaranteed salary.

CHAPTER 5

How I Got Started: A Look Back

My move to Los Angeles launched the next phase of my career. Before I continue with the Hollywood journey perhaps I should go back to where my passionate interest in show business started.

When I was fourteen, my father took me to the Metropolitan Opera in New York to see my first opera, *Die Walkure*. The stars were the reigning Wagnerians of the twentieth century, Kirsten Flagstad and Lauritz Melchior (whom I actually worked with some years later). I was enthralled by the glorious sounds, the visual opulence of the gold and red theater interior and, of course, with Wagner. I couldn't sing. I couldn't play an instrument. But I wanted to be a part of it.

Even before that catalyzing moment, I had enjoyed going to movies and the theater. But that night at the opera solidified my determination to be in show business.

I saw my first film when my aunt took me to the silent *The Count of Monte Cristo*, with Douglas Fairbanks. I was seven years old, and I still remember the moment that impressed me most: it was when Fairbanks jumped into the sea and the screen suddenly turned green. The colored filter made it seem as if the hero, and the audience with him, were really underwater.

Later, after the talkies came in, my favorites were the films of George Cukor (like Garbo's *Camille*) and Ernst Lubitsch (*Ninotchka*, with Garbo, and *The Shop Around the Corner*, with Margaret Sullivan and James Stewart.) Lubitsch had a wonderful sense of comedy and Cukor's style was very elegant.

I saw a lot of movies. In the little town on Long Island where I lived, there were two theaters that changed the double bill twice a week. That meant I could watch as many as eight pictures a week, and sometimes I managed to catch all of them.

My mother also took me to the theater. The first play I remember was a summer stock production of Kaufman and Ferber's *Dinner at Eight* in

Long Beach, Long Island. I was twelve. Later, at Broadway's Booth Theater, I remember Edmund Gwenn and Melville Cooper in *Laburnum Grove*, a play by J.B. Priestley.

When I was a teen, I worked delivering flowers during summer vacations. I spent all my earnings on theater tickets. I would buy the cheapest seats so I could see more shows. In those days, the second balcony would usually be fifty-five cents. Unfortunately, I didn't see the great Noel Coward and Gertrude Lawrence, or Alfred Lunt and Lynn Fontanne, until some years later, as their lowest ticket price was $1.65.

I loved to go to opening nights and would sneak backstage just to see the actors up close. I'd even get autographs. When I was a little older and dating, I'd go dutch with a girlfriend who was also theater-struck.

My mother pushed me academically and, although I was only sporadically a good student, I was skipped ahead a few times in school. I ended up finishing high school when I was sixteen and a half. My family had moved back into Manhattan just before my fifteenth birthday, so I graduated from George Washington High School on 192nd Street.

On the subway one day, coming home from school, my friend Leo Marks first told me about the Carolina Playmakers, the first regional theater in the country. Leo, who was the head of the high school drama club, was planning to go to college at the University of North Carolina, the home of the Playmakers. Thomas Wolfe was on the faculty at UNC, and the star of the drama faculty was Paul Green, a playwright who had recently won a Pulitzer Prize for *In Abraham's Bosom*.

It had been planned, mainly at my mother's urging, that I would attend the University of Michigan, my older brother's alma mater. But the idea of going in a different direction, literally and figuratively, of pursuing my love for the theater professionally, was a temptation I couldn't resist. I applied to UNC and was accepted. (Ironically, Leo Marks went to Harvard, and I never saw him again.)

Not yet seventeen, I left for Chapel Hill to become a Carolina Playmaker. I never played any big roles, and I don't think I was much of an actor, but I loved it all. I acted in several plays, some of them recent Broadway hits like *Room Service*. I was in *Johnny Johnson*, a play of Paul Green's that the Group Theater had just done in New York. We also did the first non-professional production of *Our Town*, Thornton Wilder's prize-winning drama.

I also helped backstage when touring companies came through Chapel Hill, a small, lovely southern village that still had the look and feel of the antebellum south. At that time, the university had only 1800 students.

Various professional musical performers would do one-night stands on the Playmakers stage, and sometimes a touring dance company would appear. Ballet was just starting to become popular in America, and I got to work backstage when Lincoln Kirstein's *Ballet Caravan* (which ultimately became the New York City Ballet) appeared.

UNC also had a radio studio, and during my senior year I wrote a

JS onstage at UNC.

radio play. It was a wartime love story and I directed the recording as my graduate thesis. In the thirties, radio was the primary form of home entertainment, so it was natural for my fellow students and me to try our hands at it. I couldn't know yet that radio would soon provide my professional entry into the arts.

While I was in college, I applied for summer jobs at the various broadcasting and theatrical venues in New York. I got some interviews, but no jobs. When I was about to graduate, I wrote again to NBC. The personnel director remembered me from an earlier interview, because when the application had asked if I typed, I said yes. That was true. But when the form asked how fast, I didn't know, so I wrote "100 words per minute." The personnel director read that and said that his secretary only typed seventy-five.

Because of that little white lie, the man remembered me a year later and I was hired — but not as a typist. Instead, I would be a page, which for decades was the standard entry-level position at NBC.

As a page, I would make only $65 a month. The network provided my uniforms and shirts, but I had to supply black shoes. I started work on July 1, 1941. Prophetically, that was the very day the Federal Communications Commission granted the first television licenses.

My first day's assignment was fabulous. I was stationed inside the famous studio 8H at NBC's glamorous Rockefeller Center. My task was to keep people out while the famed conductor Arturo Toscanini rehearsed the NBC Symphony. At that time, the symphony was composed of a hundred great musicians who had escaped Nazi Europe. On other days, I handled applause at audience shows, took tickets as audiences arrived, or brought messages to actors. I was having a wonderful time.

Five months after I joined NBC, the Japanese bombed Pearl Harbor. In retrospect, I was very fortunate that the war didn't interrupt my fledgling career, although I didn't feel that way at the time. My brother had already enlisted, and I tried to join the navy, but they rejected me. I had a bad back. Later I was drafted by the Army, but rejected again for the same reason.

So I continued to work every day or night, sometimes on the midnight shift, and learned about radio broadcasting. Some days I was stationed on the studio floors, taking messages for the actors. Many of them soon became famous. Richard Widmark was the lead on *Young Doctor Malone*. Jennifer Jones (still using her real name, Phyllis Isley) and her husband at the time, Robert Walker, were regular radio performers.

For shows that had a live audience, I handled applause. I would stand on the side of the stage and as the guests finished performing a number, I would signal the audience to applaud by raising my hands and clapping.

One night on the *Bell Telephone Hour*, the guest star was famous opera and movie star Grace Moore. As she finished singing the aria from *Madama Butterfly*, "Un Bel Di," I signaled to the audience to applaud. Miss Moore was taking a curtsy, and when she looked up she saw what I was doing.

"Get the fuck off the stage," she hissed. "If they don't want to applaud, they don't have to!" I was stunned to hear that word coming from this angelic-looking lady. Hey, I was just doing my job.

I was a green kid, barely out of my teens, and my page days were full of little learning experiences like that. On one occasion, I stood in the lobby of the 8th floor studios, announcing to the audience as they exited the elevators: "Guests of Lever Brothers' Palmolive Party, starring Barry Wood and Patsy Kelly, this way please." A well-dressed gentleman came up behind me and whispered in my ear: "It's *LEEVER* Brothers." I corrected my pronunciation of the sponsor's name in a hurry. Even at that stage of my career, the sponsor was always right!

After my first year as a page, NBC promoted me to a guide. Now I was making $85 a month. I wore the same uniform as I walked the halls of Rockefeller Center, but now it sported a different color braid.

As a guide, I took audiences who had paid for a tour of NBC around the radio facilities, giving them an inside look at how their favorite radio programs were made. I demonstrated how the sound effects were created, and put them in front of a television camera to show them how they looked on a monitor. It was a preview of the prominence television would soon have in their lives, and in mine.

The tube that made television possible was invented by Philo T. Farnsworth, who first conceived of it when he was fourteen years old. That was in 1920, the year I was born, so you might say that television and I are the same age. I had first seen television at the New York World's Fair in 1939. The elaborate demonstration in the RCA exhibit was intended to sell the television sets that the company was just beginning to make.

The Radio Corporation of America was headed by the brilliant and egocentric David Sarnoff. RCA owned the National Broadcasting Company, my future employer, which had two radio networks, the Red and the Blue. They had moved from the smaller studios at 711 Fifth Avenue to the very modern Rockefeller Center in 1932 when the multi-block complex was finished.

Sarnoff had come to the United States as a boy and worked for the Marconi company. Marconi had invented radio around the beginning of the century. He brought his invention to England and then opened a branch in the United States. Sarnoff saw the future potential of radio in the home, and created the electronics company RCA. By 1939, he understood that a visual medium could supplant radio, and hoped to begin selling a lot of RCA television sets.

Though the first television stations were first licensed for operation by the FCC in early 1941, Sarnoff's plans were stymied by the war. Since the World's Fair, RCA had sold about five thousand sets. But once RCA went to work for the war effort, the production of television sets was not resumed until 1945. In the interim, though, those of us who were around at NBC could sense the anticipation. We knew that television would soon be a big deal.

During the war years, I continued to move upward at NBC. I went from the Guest Relations department to the International Division, which had been affiliated with the government's Office of War Information. There I announced the news and disc jockeyed the latest tunes to the troops overseas. My colleagues did overseas news broadcasts in several languages.

Then NBC transferred me to the Press Department, where I learned a lot about publicity from Syd Eiges, the man in charge. Despite all the promotions, I don't think my salary had been raised very much, but I enjoyed working and learning and living in New York during the war years.

I had gotten to know a lot of people at the company and when a colleague, Bob Stevens, told me he was leaving his job as an assistant director for the Blue Network to be a director at CBS, I went to see about getting his job. The hiring manager was Ray Knight, a radio veteran performer who was now a network executive. I went to see his secretary, who told me that there were twenty people ahead of me who had applied to see Knight about the job.

I asked the secretary what I could do to get to the head of the list. She replied: "Well, you could come home with me tonight." I did. And I got the job! She and I remained good friends for many years.

About that time, the Blue Network was sold and although it continued to broadcast from the same studios and offices in Rockefeller Plaza, it became known as the American Broadcasting Company — ABC. The Red Network became the National Broadcasting Company — NBC.

In my new job as an assistant radio director, I timed the show, helping the director stick to the allotted minutes. I also made sure that no prohibited language was used, and, in general served as an ever-present representative for ABC. In those days, the top directors were usually hired by the advertising agencies. Therefore the director's loyalty tended to belong to the sponsor, whereas the assistant director's was to the network.

I first worked on a half-hour drama, *Appointment With Life*. Mark Goodson, who years later became a multimillionaire game show producer, was the director. I also assisted on *The Listening Post*, a four-times-weekly program which dramatized current stories in *The Saturday Evening Post*, the popular magazine. The *Post* featured very good writers, and many of the stories were later made into feature films. That was the case with the first one I directed for them.

The Listening Post was run by a one man producer/director/account executive, Henry Cline. One day Henry said to me: "I have to go see the client in Philadelphia tomorrow. Would you like to direct the show?" Of course, I said yes.

It seemed a monumental chore at the time, but compared to the television shows that followed a few years later, directing my first radio half-hour was very simple. One thing that made it easy was the stock company of the best actors in radio: Ethel Owen, Nancy Douglass, Brett Morrison, Everett Sloane, Myron McCormick. They were hand-selected by Henry Cline. They worked on other shows too, and Sloane was in several films and plays during the same period.

My segment was a dramatization of a short story by Harlan Ware, called "Too Young To Know." It later became a Warner Bros. film, with Joan Leslie and Robert Hutton.

I did an adequate job and could now call myself a director, but I didn't get to do another *Listening Post*. Soon after, Henry Cline took the show away from the New York branch of MacFarland Aveyard, the Chicago-based advertising agency that handled it, and went with it to their competitor, Batten, Barton, Durstine & Osborne. But the Mac-Farland Aveyard people in Chicago liked me and asked me to take over their radio department.

That sounded like an impressive job, especially for a twenty-five year-old, but in actuality MacFarland's radio output consisted of one newscast for the National Board of Fire Underwriters. Nevertheless, I decided to take the job. I left NBC and immediately began plotting to turn Mac-Farland Aveyard's little news program into a dramatic one. I hired two writers, Fred Methot and Don Agar, and together we created *Crimes of Carelessness*, a series of half-hour dramatizations of famous fires. Mac-Farland sold our idea to the client, pitching it as an exciting drama with a public service message.

Crimes of Carelessness went on Sunday afternoons over 300 stations of the Mutual network (including station WOR in New York). We had great casts and wonderful sound effects. I was both producer and director, and was able to hire the radio actors I knew as well as actors I saw on Broadway and wanted to work with. I was beginning to develop a talent pool upon which I would draw during future assignments.

For twenty six weeks I was the man in charge. And The National Board of Fire Underwriters took advantage of the popularity of *Crimes of Carelessness*, and often featured national figures speaking on fire prevention during the commercial time. But the show died after six months when the agency closed its New York office. For the first time in my adult life, I was out of a job.

However, I must have impressed the people at WOR, because I was offered, and accepted, a job as their program manager. It meant that, instead of directing a single show, I would be supervising all of WOR's New York-originated programs. Most of these were daytime talk shows designed to appeal to women, not unlike some of the morning and afternoon programs of today. There were often guest interviews with stars arranged by PR people who were plugging current plays, films, or books. The hosts were people like Martha Deane, John B. Gambling, Mike (Wallace) and Buff (Cobb, his then-wife), and Dick and Dorothy. The latter were actually Richard Kollmar, a Broadway producer and actor, and his wife Dorothy Kilgallen, the newspaper gossip columnist. Together they hosted a show called *Breakfast with Dorothy and Dick*, which was ostensibly broadcast from their Park Avenue apartment.

One day I was called into the office of Ted Streibert, the head honcho at WOR. Ted told me that he would have to let me go. "Why did you send Dorothy that nasty note?" he asked.

It seemed that someone had written unflatteringly of the Kollmar children, who were regulars on their parents' broadcast. I told Streibert that he must be mistaken, because I was very careful about sending them any unflattering mail. He suggested that I call Dorothy's sister, Eleanor who worked for the couple's agent Mark Hannah, (Eleanor later became an influential agent at MCA).

Eleanor listened to my story and then told me to hold the line while she checked the wastebasket. She found the crumpled paper and realized that it was not the letter that had been sent to me, but a carbon copy with someone else's penciled notes criticizing the Kollmar children.

I kept my job, and the next day I found on my desk a huge box from a florist shop. Inside was an olive branch wired with hundreds of olives, and a card reading: "I believe the name of that song is '*What can I say, dear, after I say I'm sorry?*' Signed, Dorothy."

In ensuing years, my name was favorably mentioned in her newspaper column on many occasions. My supervisor on all of this was Rodney Erickson and I was ecstatic when he asked me to return to directing after he moved to Young & Rubicam and began producing *We, the People*.

My first visit to Los Angeles came during the war. I worked at NBC in the short wave section broadcasting news and music to servicemen overseas. I was invited to Hollywood for the first time in the summer of 1944. A former page boy and friend, Keith Brown, was working there and I went to visit him. He introduced me to life at Peyton Hall, an apartment complex where he lived. I rented a room over the swimming pool for $20 a month. Those were the days! Susan Hayward and Jess Barker lived there, and Stella Adler was visiting with her daughter Ellen from New York. It was very glamorous.

I had a lovely affair with a young woman named Janet Lord, who lived in the building. I met Jill Warren, who wrote about Hollywood, and we became long-lasting friends. She took me to the elite Hollywood premiere of *Since You Went Away* and she introduced me to movie stars like Joan Crawford. Jill also arranged for me to go watch the filming of *A Tree Grows in Brooklyn* on the Fox back lot. This was Elia Kazan's first film. I remember ten year-old Peggy Ann Garner doing a scene with James Dunn, who played her loving, yet unsuccessful, dad. I got to direct both of them in New York on live television in the next decade.

Through Ethel Owen, one of the regulars on *The Listening Post* (the radio show I was assistant directing in New York), I met her daughter Pamela Britton, who was making a film with Frank Sinatra and Gene Kelly called *Anchors Aweigh*. I got to go to MGM to watch her film. I met Pamela's agent on the set, and she asked me if I was an actor. I said I wanted to be, so I could learn more about directing. I had not yet learned anything about acting techniques but auditioned for the studio's casting director, Lillian Burns, and she offered me a stock contract at $150 a week. Sylvia Hollow, the agent, thought the offer was too low and said if she got me into a play in New York she could get me $350 a week.

Slightly terrified of the whole prospect, I went along with the return to New York. Sylvia never got me a play and I didn't move to Hollywood until 1955. I did go back for a summer trip in 1946, when I got a chance to visit my friend Geraldine Brooks, who was shooting the film *Cry Havoc* with Barbara Stanwyck. But by then I was already directing radio and had given up my thoughts of acting. Geraldine's sister, Gloria Stroock, was spending the summer with her and when we both returned to New York I was able to cast her in my radio show *Crimes of Carelessness*. Gloria and I are still friends. Sadly, Geraldine passed away in 1977.

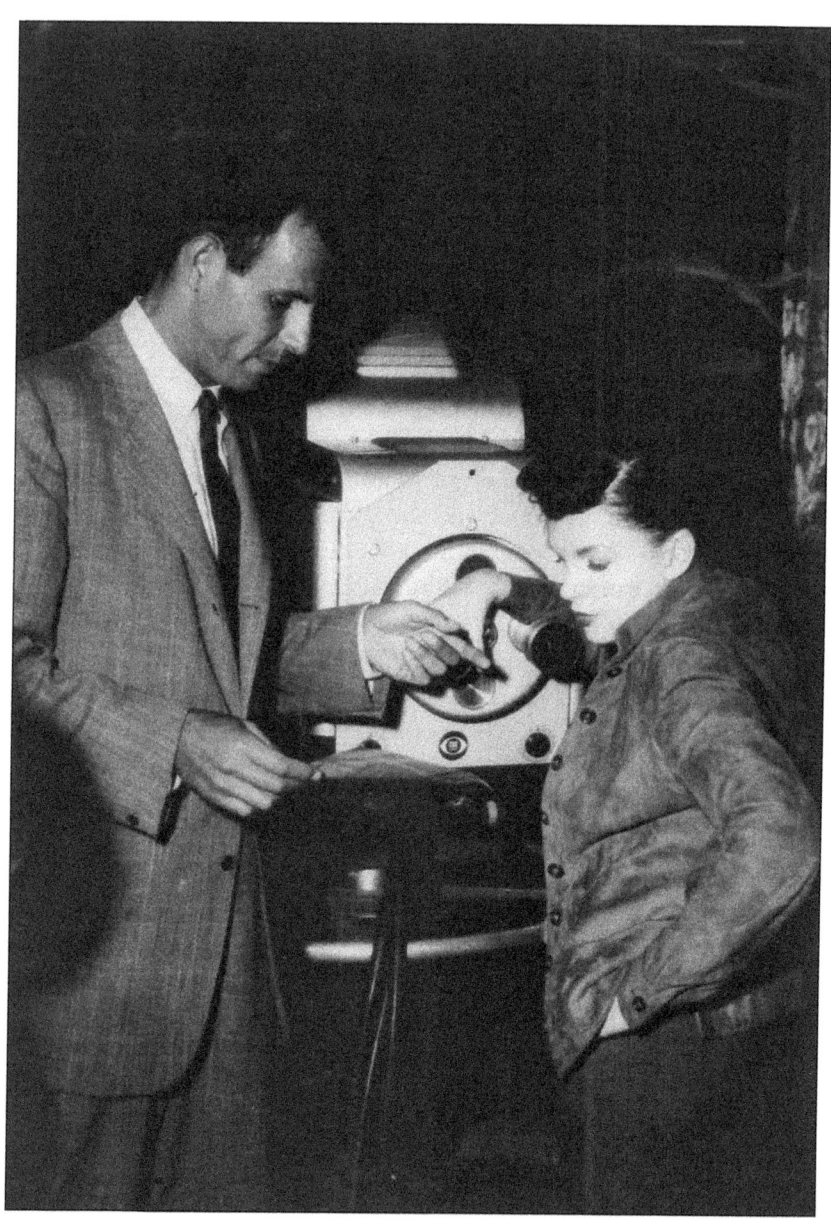

JS and Judy Garland.

CHAPTER 6

CBS, Hollywood: The Move West and Live to Film

In March 1955, my family and I moved to Los Angeles. Arthur and Adele Franz found us temporary quarters in Laurel Canyon, in a house that we sublet from director Marc Daniels, another television director who had relocated from New York. The Laurel Canyon home was a convenient home base while we looked for a more permanent place. It wasn't far from CBS, where I would be working. CBS's new and very modern Television City was next door to the storied Farmers Market, a Los Angeles landmark that I had enjoyed visiting eleven years before, on my first trip to California, and that still exists today.

Perhaps I expected to be invited to visit the homes of the people for whom I worked. I wasn't. But we made friends, slowly. My first show, *Professional Father*, was a live situation comedy starring Steve Dunne, Barbara Billingsley (who later played Beaver's mother on *Leave It to Beaver*), and a delightful child actress named Beverly Washburn. Bob Schiller, soon to be a staffer on *I Love Lucy*, was the supervising writer. *Professional Father* was pleasant enough, but it was not another *Mister Peepers*.

I was assigned other chores while I was under contract to CBS. One I was particularly fond of was doing promotional spots with Judy Garland. I presume these were for her forthcoming variety show, but that didn't actually start until later. In person Judy was nervous and stalled when she could, but no matter what she did I was delighted to be working with her. Having been a fan of hers for so many years, it was great just directing even a thirty second announcement. I didn't do much, but at least I'm able to say that I worked with Judy Garland. And when I told Liza Minnelli about this many years later, she gave me a big kiss. A publicity photo of the two of us has always been on display in my home.

Then I was assigned to Nat Perrin, who was producing a half-hour variety show with a new young comic named Johnny Carson. At that time, Carson was no more than a talented boy from Nebraska, and CBS was still searching for the right vehicle to showcase his dry wit. I still remember directing a funny skit with Johnny in gym shorts on a treadmill.

I directed for another live dramatic anthology, *Front Row Center*. My first hour was an adaptation of the familiar *The Barretts of Wimpole Street*. I had seen the play on stage, with Katherine Cornell and Brian Aherne, as well as the movie with Norma Shearer and Frederic March. I was delighted with the casting of Geraldine Fitzgerald, who I had directed the year before on the *Robert Montgomery Presents* episode "Love Story." This splendid Irish actress wouldn't fly and came all the way out to Los Angeles on the train. We met to discuss the show in a house on the beach that Geraldine had rented with her husband and young daughter.

She told me she had discussed the part with Sanford Meisner, the famous acting teacher, in New York. Meisner had told Geraldine that she was perfect for the role as long as she didn't play it as a strong Irish washerwoman. I concurred. I reminded her that Elizabeth Barrett was frail, and often ill.

That was the plan until we were actually on the air live, and the actress playing Elizabeth Barrett's sister, Henrietta, forgot her lines. Geraldine was so anxious to save the day that she covered for the other actress, and Elizabeth became much stronger than we had intended. I went out on the set during the commercial following Act One. (By 1955, commercials were seldom part of the show director's job. They'd become much more elaborate, with budgets bigger than the shows themselves. A separate commercial director, working closely with representatives of the ad agency and the client, oversaw them during the broadcast.) I reminded Geraldine of what Sandy Meisner had said. She went back to being the fragile poet, and gave a perfect performance for the rest of the show.

My CBS-Hollywood experience was a good one. It introduced me to West Coast producers like Nat Perrin, Hal Hudson, and Buck Houghton, all of whom would hire me in the future after I went freelance. It also allowed me time to visit movie studios and observe how film directing was both the same as and different from live television. Mark Stevens, an actor with whom I had worked on *Armstrong Circle Theater*, was directing a film series for television and he let me come and observe. Watching how it was actually done answered a lot of my questions about directing film.

Los Angeles was a place where work often materialized out of social connections, and I began to become a part of the Hollywood scene. Millard Kaufman was a writer friend of Arthur Laurents, and he was currently writing *Raintree County* for Elizabeth Taylor at MGM. Kaufman had written the screenplay for *Bad Day at Black Rock*, a tough, Spencer Tracy movie that was then in current release. He invited me to the commissary at MGM for lunch and showed me around the studio where I had almost been under contract a decade before. My friend Ralph Levy, who had been the first camera director on *We, the People*, was now directing both Burns and Allen's and Jack Benny's weekly television shows. One night he invited my wife and me to dinner at the Chateau Marmont Hotel, where he lived. The other dinner guests were the stars of Ralph's shows: George Burns and Gracie Allen, and Jack Benny, along with his wife Mary Livingston.

Anthony Perkins was also staying at the Marmont while he was filming *Friendly Persuasion*, William Wyler's epic about a family of pacifist Quakers during the Civil War. When we had lunch, Tony offered me a job directing his next film, in which he would be the star. It was the story of baseball player Jim Piersall, whose career was interrupted by mental illness. I had not yet done any work on film, and modestly told Tony thank you, but that I'd like to learn more about film before I direct one. It was a stupid decision. The director he did choose for the Piersall movie, *Fear Strikes Out*, was Bob Mulligan, another live television veteran who also had not done any film when he said yes to Tony's offer. Mulligan went on to more features and considerable acclaim. I vowed to accept the next offer.

At CBS, the production chief who hired me, Bill Dozier, had left television to head feature film production at RKO. Without Dozier as an ally, I wasn't getting the dramatic assignments I wanted. I decided to freelance again. And there was plenty of work.

My first TV film was for producer Richard Irving at Revue, a company owned by MCA. Music Corporation of America, originally a band-booking outfit in the twenties, was one of the largest talent agencies in the film industry, and at the time I was one of its clients. Irving was impressed with my New York background, my knowledge of theater and of actors, and my previous credits. Revue was headquartered then at the Republic Studios in Studio City, which was still run by the founder of Republic Pictures, Herbert B. Yates. Yates had seen the future of television and wasn't fighting it, unlike the major studios. In the mid-fifties, Revue was producing half-hour films for use on a variety of different anthology series, and the first teleplays I directed there were for MCA-packaged shows like *Studio 57* and *Jane Wyman Presents the Fireside Theater*.

Meanwhile, the producer Hal Hudson had left CBS and was producing the *Zane Grey Theater* for Four Star. Four Star was a company formed by a quartet of movie stars no longer under contract to studios:

Dick Powell, David Niven, Charles Boyer, and Ida Lupino. They were the company's owners (Powell was the one who really ran things) and they took turns lending their name value to the *Four Star Playhouse*, a weekly anthology not unlike the shows I was doing at Revue. *Zane Grey Theater* was a sort of follow-up to the *Four Star Playhouse*, a western anthology named after the well-known writer of western novels. Dick Powell appeared on screen, in western garb and with prop lassos and saddles and such, to introduce each week's episode.

I didn't know much about westerns, but I plunged in. My first show was headlined by the movie star Robert Ryan, and scripted by a young writer named Christopher Knopf. I helped Knopf on the script revisions, and the show later won him awards. It was called "Interrogation."

Zane Grey filmed on a tight schedule. Typically, the first day was location day for all the exterior filming, and then we had another two days on the sound stage. Having had no experience with westerns or horses, I felt a bit insecure with the crew. I confided this to Ryan after observing his impressive ability to ride and, in particular, to stop in just the right spot to hit his mark for the camera. Ryan said that I should see the films of the director Anthony Mann. Ryan told me that Mann was good with actors, as I was, but also very good at directing action. That weekend, I saw *The Tin Star*, Mann's latest feature film. In it, Henry Fonda teaches Anthony Perkins how to "cock it on the draw" as he pulls his gun.

The following week, I directed another *Zane Grey Theater*. This time the star was Eddie Albert, with whom I had worked in New York. The first shot of the day on location had to be a medium shot of Eddie, as the morning fog had not yet lifted enough to shoot the wider master shot. As the action began, Eddie pulled his gun. I said "Cut!"

Then, very authoritatively, I said, "No, Ed, you've gotta *cock it on the draw!*" I could feel the crew snap to attention. This city slicker must know what he's doing, after all. I felt comfortable with them after that!

I directed other *Zane Grey* episodes, and the one I remember most fondly starred Barbara Stanwyck. Stanwyck, a leading lady of many film dramas and comedies, was now working mainly in television. In her episode of *Zane Grey* she played the mother of three children in the Old West. Many years later, in New York, I was invited to a tribute to Stanwyck by the wife of the head of the Film Society of Lincoln Center, Joanne Melniker Stern. Joanne had been an entertainment editor on *Look* magazine and knew that I had worked with "Missy," as people who knew her called Stanwyck. After the ceremony in Avery Fisher Hall, which included speeches by the celebrants and clips from Stanwyck's films, I rode up in the elevator to the dining room with William Holden and Frank Capra. It was that kind of an evening.

Upstairs, Joanne Stern insisted I get on the greeting line where Stanwyck was greeting guests. I tried to beg off, but Joanne insisted. I didn't think Stanwyck would remember me, but she did.

"I'll bet you don't remember what I said to you," Stanwyck recalled. "In the scene where the Indians were coming, I hugged the kids in front of me and you said I'd protect them more behind me. And I said, "No, because I hated those kids." I had forgotten. She hadn't.

I chatted briefly with Stanwyck that night. She said she was surprised when the Film Society called her about this tribute. At first, she thought they wanted Barbra *Streisand*. As we were talking, Stanwyck noticed William Holden across the room.

"You see that fellow over there?" Stanwyck asked. "People talk about how cold-hearted Hollywood people are. On April 1, 1939, Bill Holden and I started shooting on *Golden Boy*. It was his first picture, so I worked with him between setups, whenever we had free time. He was very appreciative. I just wanted the picture to be good. I was the star. Since then, every April 1, I get a dozen white roses. He knew I liked them. I have been getting a dozen white roses every year for almost fifty years." Her eyes teared. Sadly, this was to be the last time, as Holden died the following year when he fell and struck his head while at home alone, possibly under the influence of alcohol.

I had met playwright Jerome Lawrence in New York when his hit play *Auntie Mame*, starring Rosalind Russell, was the big hit of the theater season. He had seen a *Robert Montgomery Presents* that I had directed. An actor friend of his, Bill Lundmark, had played opposite ex-child star Peggy Ann Garner. Jerry was impressed with my direction. He and his writing partner, Robert E. Lee, had secured the rights to a television series about the U. S. Military Academy at West Point. Supposedly, the officers' wives wanted house seats for *Auntie Mame*, and Jerry struck a deal. When I moved west and began directing television films, Jerry introduced me to Maurice "Babe" Unger, the head of production for the Ziv Company, which was producing the *West Point Story* series. I was hired to direct every other episode.

Leon Benson produced *West Point Story* and directed some episodes. We filmed the exteriors at the actual military academy north of New York City, and the interiors in Hollywood. We would shoot six shows at a time; usually the outdoor location scenes for all six would be scheduled together, and then the two directors would return to Los Angeles to film the interiors at the Ziv Studios on Santa Monica Boulevard in Hollywood. I had never done a distant location show before. Each half hour was shot on a tight two day per episode schedule, and if we didn't finish a scene, a line of narration covered the omission.

The scripts were written so that only the lead actors would be working on both coasts. We would cast them in Hollywood, and the parts that only played on location were cast out of New York. I recommended my friend, the agent Jane Deacy, and her office did the eastern casting. I was pleased to be able to return the favor Jane did for me when she introduced me to Fred Coe. I kept her as my agent on the *Mister Peepers* deal, even though I had been asked by David Susskind to let him handle me. My loyalty to Jane meant that David never hired me on any of his shows after he became one of the top television producers in New York.

There were no running characters in *West Point Story* except for the "host cadet," a typical young soldier played by actor Donald May. The Military Academy supplied real cadets for use as extras, as well as authentic uniforms, technical advice, and of course their facilities as our primary location. It was a great deal for Ziv, although there were rules we had to follow.

When on Academy grounds all actors had to behave like cadets. They had to keep their collars buttoned. They couldn't smoke, and had to stand at attention when officers passed. As far as the military was concerned, they were cadets when they were there and were to behave accordingly. Many of the actors disliked this and there were many minor infractions of the rules. One actor was so upset he threw up.

Another rule had to do with height. Cadets were assigned to their platoons according to size, so that in a given platoon everyone was the same height, whether they were 5'5" or 6'6". If two actors played roommates, they had to be the same height. I got to be very adept at judging heights when interviewing actors, even without asking. Once, I cast a script about a plane crash, in which two skiing cadets rescue one of their fathers from a private plane that has crashed on a mountain near the Academy. We had cast Jerome Courtland, with whom I had worked on Broadway in *Bus Stop*, in the lead. Jerome was 6'5", and we had to find someone just as tall to play his roommate. A handsome six-foot-fiver walked into the office and I asked him, "Do you ski?" He said yes, and I gave him the part. The young man was Clint Eastwood.

Some days later, as we were filming at the location, I sketched out to the cast how the scene would be staged. "You two start at the top of that mountain and ski down here to the plane," I said to Jerome and Clint.

The plane was a mock-up which we had stuck in the snow. "When you reach the plane, start to open the door and I will cut. Then the camera will move in and we'll cover it closer. When you're coming down the slope, stay close together."

Eastwood came up to me and said, "I can't do that."

"You said you could ski," I replied.

Sheepishly, he responded, "I needed the job."

There we were, assembled on the side of a mountain, deep in snow, with the light fading fast. It was winter and dusk ended our shooting day before five in the afternoon. There was no provision in the budget for stunt doubles. I did have a technical advisor from the Academy who could ski, but he was not 6'5" tall.

Quickly, I came up with a plan using my technical advisor in place of Clint. "The two of you start at the top," I said. "Jerry, you get ahead of him so we don't notice the height difference. The camera will pan with Jerry, and when he reaches this spot on level ground near the plane, Clint, you ski in from off camera." It worked. Clint was grateful that I hadn't fired him, or let it be known that his white lie had almost cost us a crucial shot. And when the film was shown, no one noticed that Clint couldn't ski. Necessity, as they say, is the mother of invention.

Larry Hagman had his first television role on *West Point Story*. Jane Deacy had said to me that she had a wonderful, unknown actor for a particular part. She also told me that the young man insisted no one was to know who his mother was. At the time, one of the two reigning musical stars on Broadway was Mary Martin. (The other was Ethel Merman.) Larry was Mary's son, but he wanted to make it on his own. He was splendid in the part. After he had established himself on television's *I Dream of Jeannie*, Larry didn't mind if people knew about his famous lineage. We worked again, years later, in his *Dallas* days, when he played the eccentric oil millionaire J.R. In between Larry's two series, we palled around a bit when we both lived on Malibu Beach. I was happy to see that his marriage to Mai was still a happy one. We'd often walk on the beach and chat.

I had a wonderful assistant director on *West Point Story*. He was the son of the famous actor/director, Erich von Stroheim. Erich, Jr., was very tall, but resembled his dad down to the bald head. He was very efficient, but unfortunately he lacked a sense of humor. I kidded him once when we were shooting an episode where two cadets are crossing the Hudson River in a rowboat. This is no mean feat under the best of circumstances. The story specified that the cadets had trouble with the breaking ice flow coming down the river. There were very visible large pieces of real ice floating down at this season of the year. Joking, I said, "Erich, would you please have the ice come closer to the rowboat."

Not catching on that I was kidding, Erich complained loudly about the fact that he only had one assistant and no other boats were supplied, that this wasn't the MGM back lot, and so on. We loved him, though, and felt safe when he was handling the schedules and the crew and all the things a good assistant director does.

West Point was just a couple of hours drive from Manhattan, and if you weren't shooting at night you could catch a Broadway show. Ethel Merman, the reigning musical comedy star, was in appearing in *Happy Hunting* that season. My brother had lent me his car, and some of the cast wanted a ride into the city with me. I was tired after a long day of filming, so when one of our actors, Eddie Foy IV (of the famous theatrical Foy family) volunteered to drive, I agreed. During the ride, I said, "Not so fast, Eddie, we don't want to be stopped for speeding."

It was around the third time I warned him that we got stopped by the police. We were already in Manhattan, heading south on the West Side Highway. Eddie pulled over. The cop pulled up behind us and walked up to the car. "Let me see your license," he said.

Eddie, it turned out, didn't have a license. "Okay," tried the police officer, "Let me see the ownership license."

I hadn't gotten that document from my brother. "You boys are coming with me," the cop said.

Eddie, who wasn't coming to the show with me, pleaded, "Officer, take us in, but could you let him grab a cab? He has tickets for Ethel Merman tonight."

"Ethel Moiman, huh?" said our Runyonesque police officer. He thought it over. "Okay."

And he hailed me a taxi and I ended up at the theater just as the curtain was going up. All New Yorkers loved Ethel Merman. My brother's car, and Eddie, ended up at the station house. His father, Eddie Foy III, was appearing in *The Pajama Game* on Broadway, and he was summoned after the show to get Eddie and his other passengers released. I got the ownership papers from my brother, and we made it back to West Point in time to catch some sleep before starting the next day's shooting.

I got to work on other Ziv shows. They were all basically the same: low-budget action shows with the emphasis on novel locations instead of the stories. *West Point Story* only lasted for one year, but the following summer Leon Benson and I alternated directing on another Ziv series, this one filmed in San Francisco. *Harbor Command* starred Wendell Corey, with whom I had worked on *Robert Montgomery Presents*. In those days, we filmed six days a week, and would get three episodes in the can each week. (Some years later, union rules mandated a five-day work week.)

I enjoyed that summer of '57, living in San Francisco and commuting back to Los Angeles for casting sessions and family visits. As on *West Point Story*, if any scenes weren't finished within the allotted two days, narration would be inserted to keep the story straight. Going over two days was not an option. This impossible schedule was even more impossible on *Harbor Command* than on *West Point Story* because Wendell Corey had a drinking problem. Not only was I with him all day filming, but at night I would stick by him to make sure he got back to the hotel to sleep it off in time for his call the next day. Wendell never missed a line or a shot, but he did like his booze.

Babe Unger had struck a deal to use the resources of the San Francisco Harbor Command, just as he had done with the Military Academy. We spent several days a week shooting in San Francisco bay, on the Harbor Command boat. The show looked fantastic, no matter which way we turned the camera it was a great shot. Extensive location shooting, like we were using on *Harbor Command*, was ahead of its time. As television reception improved, and viewers became more sophisticated, there was more of a demand for realistic locations instead of phony back lots.

Ziv's frugality and back-breaking schedules meant that, instead of established professionals, a lot of young, inexperienced people like myself got their start on those half-hour adventure shows. Jon Epstein and Quinn Martin, both of whom became important producers and later hired me to direct their shows, had their basic training at Ziv. Quinn was a sound editor in the post-production facility, and Jon was Babe Unger's assistant. Gene Roddenberry was a Los Angeles policeman who served as the technical advisor on *Highway Patrol*, a popular Ziv police series with Broderick Crawford. Gene wanted to try his hand at writing and Unger gave him a crack at it. He wrote some successful *Highway Patrol*s and used that credit to leave the police force and launch himself as a freelance writer. Later, of course, Roddenberry became famous, and very wealthy, as the creator of *Star Trek*. The Ziv organization was a great training ground.

CHAPTER 7

The Millionaire, The Donna Reed Show and Death Valley Days: Dramas, Comedies and Westerns

"James Sheldon has been signed by Columbia Pictures Screen Gems to direct seven episodes of Celebrity Playhouse *and* Ford Theater.*"*
NEW YORK TIMES, APRIL 1956

Some of the filmed anthologies that I was directing in the late fifties were produced at Screen Gems, the television arm of Columbia Pictures. I was contracted for a certain number of half-hour dramas for *Celebrity Playhouse* and *Ford Theater*. At other studios, when a scene began, an assistant cameraman would use the clapboard, the familiar black-and-white chalkboard you've seen in the movies. As soon as the director hears the clack, he says, "Action." The sound of the clack was there to synchronize camera and sound for the editing process. On the film, the sound track is seven frames behind the picture.

At Screen Gems, instead of the standard handheld clapboard, they used one that was built into the camera. When I started at Screen Gems, I found myself waiting for the sound clap without realizing it. One of my first films there starred Joanne Dru and my friend Arthur Franz. For a climactic scene, I had lined up a close camera shot of their two heads, with his hands strangling her bent body. Silence. After a pause, Arthur looked up and said, "Say Action!"

Of course, I said it and the scene started. I don't think I forgot again. Clint Eastwood, when he directs, never says action. He says something less intrusive and more soothing to his actors at the beginning of a scene. Perhaps he had an experience like mine during his early years in television.

Ford Theater allowed me to work with some major actors. The stage and screen star Brian Aherne did one, as did Eugenie Leontovich, fresh from her success on Broadway as the Empress in *Anastasia*. I had heard she was difficult, but she was very much the opposite. When I suggested a move, Leontovich said, "Whatever my director wants."

I was directing another episode with Frank Lovejoy in May, 1956, when my second son was born. The title of that segment was "Sweet Charlie," and I suggested that we name our son after the show. But my wife liked Anthony better than Charles, and she pointed out if we named him John and made Anthony his middle name, his initials would be an abbreviation of my first name. So we named my second and last child John Anthony Sheldon, and he's called Tony.

Another series I directed at Screen Gems was *The Donna Reed Show*. Donna's husband, Tony Owen, was the producer of this sitcom, in which Reed played the typical, all-American housewife and mother. We shot the interiors for *The Donna Reed Show* at the Columbia lot, on Gower Street in Hollywood, and the occasional location scenes at the Columbia ranch in Burbank, near Warner Brothers and Universal Studios.

At that time my wife and I were living in a beach house in Malibu that we had rented from the comedian Joe E. Brown. It was a long drive from there into Hollywood, but I would carpool with my next door neighbor, Bill Asher, when our schedules permitted. Bill had been the director of *I Love Lucy*. Soon, he would produce the hit comedy *Bewitched*, divorce his then-wife and marry the show's star, Elizabeth Montgomery, who I had known when she was a teenaged ingénue on her father's live anthology in New York.

In the late fifties, Bill Asher produced *The Jane Wyman Show*, an anthology half-hour hosted by Wyman after she divorced Ronald Reagan. My work day was usually from 7am to 7pm. Once, when I was driving back from the studio with Asher, we stopped for a beer at a Malibu Canyon pub and met a young would-be actor named Merle Johnson. Merle was nineteen and not at all knowledgeable about how to get his career started. Bill Asher and I both helped him, and through an introduction to the legendary agent Henry Willson, Merle became Troy Donahue. Willson was famous for rechristening beefcake stars with catchy names; for instance, he had discovered Rock Hudson (whose real name was Roy Harold Fitzgerald). Troy Donahue was no Rock Hudson, but he landed a contract at Warner Bros. and had some success as a movie heartthrob for several years. I encouraged him to study acting, but Troy told me, "I don't want to be an actor, I want to be a star." He achieved that goal while he was still young and handsome, but as he aged he had great difficulty finding work. He died too young.

While I still lived in New York, my wife and I had gone to see a play on Broadway. The reviews were not good but my friend, Lloyd Bridges, was playing the lead and I wanted to see it. I had not yet worked with Bridges, but a girlfriend of mine had gotten the lead opposite him in a play trying out in Boston. She replaced the original lead on short notice so I went along to help her learn her lines. But after two weeks in Boston, they both were replaced when *Heartsong* moved on to Philadelphia. It never got to New York. We had become friendly with the Bridges, so we went to the new play *Dead Pigeon*.

When the curtain went down, I said to my wife, "Those critics are crazy. This is a damn good play!" A bald gentleman sitting in front of me turned around and said, "Thank you very much. I wrote it."

That's how I met Leonard Kantor. We both moved west about the same time and eventually worked together on several shows. Leonard introduced me to a writer named Joe Petracca, who was working on a screenplay for Sam Goldwyn, Jr., called *The Proud Rebel*. Joe had written a collection of stories based on his family, who had emigrated from Italy to the United States to escape the famine, just after the turn of the century. I thought it would make a good television series.

Joe and I put together an hour-long pilot script and I took advantage of my contact with my old Ziv co-worker, Quinn Martin, who by 1959 was producing the *Desilu Playhouse*. This was an hour-long dramatic anthology hosted by Desi Arnaz. Quinn liked the script, and I directed the pilot, which aired on the *Playhouse*. Marisa Pavan (Oscar winner for *The Rose Tattoo* and MGM's star Pier Angeli's twin sister) and Robert Loggia played the leads. Loggia played a young Italian who immigrates to Brooklyn around 1905. He has one burning desire: to return to Sorrento and become a farmer. Marisa's character loves him, but she also loves America and wants to stay here. The conflict between their respective desires would have driven subsequent episodes of the series, had it sold.

Some years earlier, I had given Loggia his first job on a *Robert Montgomery Presents* with Jackie Cooper and Lee Remick. A friend of mine, Howard Sloan, had asked me to give his brother-in-law a job; the brother-in-law turned out to be Bob, and he was a fine actor who turned in quite a good performance. *Come Back to Sorrento*, which was our title for Joe Petracca's pilot, turned out well, too. But just as we were hoping for Quinn to sell it as a series, ABC picked up another *Desilu Playhouse* pilot, *The Untouchables*. It was a huge hit, and took all of Quinn's time. Leonard Kantor ended up writing a number of episodes of *The Untouchables*, but nothing ever came of *Come Back to Sorrento*. Leonard and I also worked together on *The Millionaire*, in the sixties for Quinn Martin again on *The Fugitive*, and a decade later on *McMillan & Wife*. We developed a close friendship, which ended too soon when diabetes took Leonard's life in the eighties.

I was a big Frank Sinatra fan and was thrilled when I was hired to direct an episode of his anthology show in the late 1950's. He occasionally appeared on the show but more often was the host and I was hired for one of the shows where he just emceed. I was on the set one day when Frank was doing a musical number. After the take, the assistant director told Frank that the boom mic had gotten in the shot and could he please do it again. Frank's response was "Blow up the shot and fire the boom man," and he walked off the set. I was surprised to see my idol acting so unprofessionally. I was glad I was not directing that day.

I had met Gower Champion, the Broadway dancer and choreographer, through Jane Deacy, his agent, some years before. As a summer replacement for the Jack Benny program, CBS had bought a half-hour live show starring Gower and his wife Marge. Ralph Levy, my TV mentor from *We, the People*, was directing the Benny show and recommended me as the director of the Champion project.

Because I knew Gower was a director as well as a choreographer, I was skeptical about accepting the job. I went to see Gower and he asked me my opinion of the first script. I told him what elements I liked, and which ones I didn't. He seemed impressed with my comments and asked me to please take the job. It would be us against the network. Liking him and knowing I could learn from this brilliant stager, I accepted.

The show was to be filmed at Revue Studios. We rehearsed the whole first show, including a big dance number. I had all my homework done and was eager to start shooting. Then, on the first day, I was driving to the studio through Laurel Canyon. Ahead there had been an accident. When I got close enough I recognized Gower's convertible MG. He was lying on the street, with paramedics tending to him. The impact of the crash was so strong that Gower's teeth cut through the skin below his lower lip. He mumbled to me, "Call Marge." I did.

With Gower's face disfigured, at least temporarily, the shoot had to be postponed. As Gower recovered in the hospital, Marge more or less took control, and the network assigned a producer to help. He didn't. By the time Gower was fully recovered, there wasn't time to film. We had to do the shows live. That limited the choreography and forced us to simplify the look of the show. For the Champions, dancing was fine, but they weren't really actors. Though they had done some musicals at MGM, they didn't come across well as actors on television.

After a short time, the producer that had been assigned when Gower was hospitalized fired me and took over the direction, which I suspected had been his intent from the beginning. It didn't make the show better. It went off the air after the summer hiatus and didn't return. I learned a lot from Gower in that short time, though. Whenever I had a difficult fight scene, I would ask myself, "How would Gower stage this?" His techniques for choreographing dance could apply just as well to staging violent action. This epiphany proved particularly helpful a few years later, when I directed a *Naked City* featuring an elaborate fight involving two butchers inside a real meat-packing house on 14th Street in Manhattan. It was a very successful episode called "King Stanislaus and the Knights of the Round Stable," with Jack Klugman and John Larch as the butchers, and even today I am pleased with what I accomplished in that pivotal fight scene.

In the late fifties, I began to direct *The Millionaire*. I had met the associate producer and sometime director of this series, Gerald Mayer, through a friend named Irvin Graham, who had been a writer on *Holiday Hotel*. Gerry introduced me to the people at Don Fedderson's production company, which produced *The Millionaire*. A fantasy about a rich man who gave away a million dollars every week, *The Millionaire* was loosely based on a Paramount picture of the thirties, *If I Had a Million*. Marvin Miller played the middle man who was given a check to deliver each week, and Paul Frees provided the voice of the millionaire, J. Beresford Tipton. We never photographed Tipton's face.

In essence an anthology, *The Millionaire* featured a variety of stars in different episodes. One of my favorite shows starred Rita Moreno and Ben Cooper. She did a splendid Puerto Rican accent, and with their shared background in theater they worked well together. That episode was written by Robert Altman, who came on the set one day. At one point, Bob pulled me aside and asked, "Who is that girl over there?" He pointed to an attractive young woman who was working as an extra. I asked Bob if he would like me to introduce them. He said yes. Bob later married that extra, and he and Helen remained together until he died almost fifty years later.

Another reason I remember that episode in particular is because I was running behind schedule and the production manager, John Stephens, was on my back. We usually filmed ten pages or more in a day. After lunch, I still had nine pages to shoot. Because I had confidence in Rita and Ben, and because I trusted the crew, I planned the whole nine pages as if it were a live television scene, done all on one camera with no cuts. The actors performed almost a whole day's work in a single take. We finished ahead of schedule. I ended up directing forty-six *Millionaire* episodes.

I had first worked with producer Nat Perrin when I was at CBS Hollywood directing the early Johnny Carson show. A couple of years later, Perrin was producing *Death Valley Days*, then hosted by Ronald

Millionaire guest Dennis Hopper.

Reagan. This was a low-budget, syndicated show produced on the shortest schedule possible: two and a half days for a half-hour show. And sometimes, they were done on location. Once, I had a tricky, ambitious *Death Valley Days* script, and I asked Perrin for more time in which to shoot it.

"Jim," he said, "let me tell you the paper battleship story. Not long ago, there was a very good play on Broadway called *Mister Roberts*, starring Henry Fonda. The theater could only gross fifty thousand a week, even if the show sold out, and they couldn't afford a real battleship. So they put up a paper battleship. The audience accepted it, loved the play. It was sold out for a year.

"So," Nat said, "give me a paper battleship."

I modified my thinking, finished the episode on schedule, and it worked. Here, too, if we didn't get to finish shooting a scene, Nat would write a hasty line of narration to tie loose ends together. The voice that spoke those lines explaining any plot points I didn't have time to shoot belonged to our future president, Ronald Reagan.

In 1958, Eleanor and I divorced and I moved out on my own. I found that in Hollywood, for a successful director, the social life of a bachelor differed from that of a married man.

Also in 1958, I was invited to the wedding of my brother's college chum, Howard Barnes, who I had admired greatly because he worked at CBS, to a woman named Molly Mock, who he had met on a plane. Howard asked me to be his best man. Molly's maid of honor was a woman named Caroline Veiller, who I ended up going out with and is still a friend. Caroline was Hollywood royalty: her father was an important screenwriter, Anthony Veiller, and her mother, the writer Laura Kerr, had married the writer Allen Rifkin after her divorce from Veiller.

Caroline (who later married the TV writer-producer Philip Saltzman) was about fifteen years younger than I was, and she introduced me to a circle of friends in her age group who were all children of well-known film industry figures. One was Mervyn LeRoy's daughter Linda, whose mother was Doris Warner (the daughter of movie mogul Harry Warner). Doris had divorced Mervyn and married the director Charles Vidor, who had a son, Michael, by his first wife, actress Karen Morley, a very popular actress in the 30s and 40s. Michael became a friend of mine as well. Also in this group were Nicola Lubitsch, the daughter of Ernst Lubitsch, and Judy Lewis, whose mother was Loretta Young and whose father was Clark Gable. Several of these people are still good friends of mine.

After Caroline, I dated Nicola and, later, Judy. It became sort of a habit that all my girlfriends were the daughters of famous filmmakers. This was mainly a coincidence, although as a movie fan and a director myself, I guess I enjoyed the connection.

Those were still the days where there was a difference between men and women, particularly in the workplace, as the current television series *Mad Men* illustrates so well.

Although a director had an agent who was supposed to keep him working, much of the job hunting was done socially. It wasn't that people liked or disliked you necessarily, but unless they needed a director, they didn't think about you, and when they found they did need a director, it was often the first one who popped into their mind who got hired. So it was necessary to socialize.

I had a nice house to entertain in and did so often. It was much easier to ask a producer to have lunch by the pool than to say, "I'm looking for work." And there were people who reciprocated and invited you to their house where there were other producers who might be looking for directors. I don't think it's different in any business, except there was more of a turnover for a freelance director in television whose assignments lasted for three weeks.

One of my favorite party-givers was a producer I worked for quite frequently, Jon Epstein. He had a regular series of parties even though he had a steady job as a producer at Universal Studios. I was always invited. His house on Coldwater Canyon had a huge party room. Jerry Lawrence, my playwright friend, was also a wonderful party giver. His house overlooked the Pacific Ocean in Malibu. I have a picture of me and Ingrid Bergman and another with Jean Arthur taken at this house.

I also threw my own parties for celebrity friends who happened to be in town, like Stella Adler. At one of those parties for her, even Marlon Brando came. At another party I had in town for Stella's eightieth birthday (she died at 93) I hired the then-undiscovered Michael Feinstein for $50 to play the piano all night.

It was not hard for me to be charming at a party, particularly if I enjoyed the people. If there was a job I really wanted I might be tongue-tied, but just being there reminded people that you were around. I guess I must have been doing it right, because I kept working steadily.

CHAPTER 8

The Twilight Zone, The Fugitive and *Route 66:* Me and Television At Our Best

If there's one show I get asked about more than any other, it's probably *The Twilight Zone*. I directed six episodes of the classic horror anthology, including the classic "It's a Good Life," the one in which Billy Mumy (the same boy who later starred in *Lost in Space*) wishes people who annoy him "into the cornfield."

I had known Rod Serling slightly in New York, but it was probably *The Twilight Zone*'s line producer, Buck Houghton, who hired me for the show. I had known Buck when I was a staff director at CBS Television City. *The Twilight Zone* was a co-production of CBS and Rod Serling's company, Cayuga Productions, and when I came onto the show during its second season Rod was in the middle of a standoff with the network. Originally CBS had wanted to tape the show on one of the empty soundstages at its Television City facility. But Rod had been firm about contracting to shoot *The Twilight Zone* on the MGM back lot. There, the show had access to considerably more production route than CBS could provide: bigger soundstages, elaborate sets left over from big-budget movies, more varied and realistic back lot locations. Now CBS was again pressuring Serling to shoot *The Twilight Zone* at its own facilities. As the ratings were not tremendous (they never were during the series' original run), Rod had acquiesced and agreed to shoot six episodes on videotape at CBS Television City. Because of my experience in live television, I was hired to direct two of those.

By 1960, electronic tape had come to the forefront. Shooting on tape was more desirable to the networks because, unlike live broadcasts, taped shows could be preserved for reruns. Tape was also cheaper than film. The down side was that early two-inch videotape was very difficult to edit. The cuts had to be made by hand, and they had to be exact. If the editor made a mistake, there was no way to fix it.

My two videotaped *Twilight Zone*s were "Long Distance Call," about a boy (Billy Mumy) who calls his dead grandmother on a toy telephone, and "The Whole Truth," in which a used car salesman (Jack Carson) found himself unable to lie. "Long Distance Call" also starred Lili Darvas, the great Hungarian theater actress who had been married to the playwright Ferenc Molnar, as the grandmother. I thought they were successful on their own terms, but Rod and Buck disliked the cramped look of the taped shows. For "The Whole Truth," we filled the soundstage with automobiles, but nothing we did could make our indoor used car lot look like an authentic outdoor location. After that initial batch of six, *The Twilight Zone* returned to the MGM back lot and to film.

Before the two videotaped *Twilight Zone* episodes, I had done one on film. "A Penny For Your Thoughts" was a straight sitcom in which Dick York played a bank clerk who could read people's minds. Dick starred as the original husband on *Bewitched* later, but he had been a wonderful actor in the theatre, too. He had studied in New York with Sanford Meisner, who I considered the best of all the famous acting teachers, especially for an actor doing television. I also directed Dick in an episode of *The Millionaire*, in which he played a vacuum cleaner salesman. There was a scene in which he had to quickly put a vacuum cleaner into the trunk of the car and drive away, but when he tried this in the first take he couldn't get the trunk open. I said, "Cut," and Dick said, "Oh, you shouldn't have cut. I had the greatest idea." The training with Meisner had taught Dick to improvise on everything, and the problem with the trunk had motivated Dick to try something very funny. He was able to recapture it in a subsequent take, but that incident taught me never to cut too quickly when a shot seemed to go awry.

"A Penny For Your Thoughts" was the first of many *Twilight Zone* scripts by George Clayton Johnson, a young, inexperienced writer who was around on the set when we shot the episode. I was able to work with George on his script and make some contributions that he thought were worthwhile. At the time, George dressed like a preppie. When I next saw him, nearly fifty years later, he looked like a mountain man, with long hair and a long white beard. At first I didn't recognize him, but we had a warm reunion and he still spoke enthusiastically about my direction of that show.

My next episode, "It's a Good Life," has become a favorite among fans. Cloris Leachman and John Larch starred as the parents of the telekinetic farm boy, but what I remember most about that episode was working a second time with Billy Mumy. He was bright, talented, and fast — a

JS and Billy Mumy on *Twilight Zone*.

perfect little boy — and we all loved working with him. His mother, contrary to the stereotype, was also just the nicest lady. Without meaning to or even realizing it, I took terrible advantage of her one day on one of Billy's *Twilight Zone*s. I needed just one more close up to finish with Billy, but it was past his stop time. I said to his mother, "Can I just get one more shot?" She said yes, and I got the shot. But then they came down on me. The production manager asked, "Do you know they could close down the studio?" I had violated the child labor law that strictly mandated how many hours a child actor could work on a movie set. I never did that again — but I got that shot on that day.

My fifth *Twilight Zone*, "Still Valley," featured Gary Merrill as the only moving actor amid a platoon of extras playing soldiers who were frozen in time. It was sort of an interesting idea, but the script was weak. My last episode, "I Sing the Body Electric," should have been another classic, as it was based on a Ray Bradbury story. But the show was troubled by production problems, which began with the casting.

In the sixties, casting directors had less power than they do today. Their job was to find good actors whose price fit the show's budget, and recommend them to the director or the producer. Some producers I worked for, like Douglas Cramer, imposed their will on the casting; others, like David Gerber or Bill D'Angelo, let the director select the actors. At times, a big star would be cast before the director was hired. But it was always understood that the final decisions rested with the director or the producer, not with the casting director. *The Twilight Zone*'s casting director, Jim Lister, usurped this authority on "I Sing the Body Electric." Lister suggested an actress named Josephine Hutchinson to play the robot grandmother who, in the story, is purchased by a recently widowed father to serve as a surrogate mother for his three children. I thought Hutchinson was all wrong for the part. She had an earthy persona, and I wanted someone lighter, with more humor, who would give the grandmother a kind of magic quality to which the children would naturally respond.

I had known Jim Lister for years — we had both been pages at NBC during the war — but that didn't stop him from using a bit of subterfuge to get Hutchinson in the part. Jim told us that the actress I wanted was not available, and I later found out that wasn't true. In the end, Hutchinson gave an adequate performance, but she was the wrong type and there was simply nothing I could do to get what I needed out of her.

What I did enjoy about "I Sing the Body Electric" was working with the children, especially the talented Veronica Cartwright. It was probably just a coincidence that three of my *Twilight Zone*s featured children in the leading roles, but I was particularly good with children's shows and would later spend a lot of time directing Don Fedderson's situation comedies, which all centered around kids. I loved working with children and developed a few techniques for getting good performances from them. A director had to "play daddy" to child actors. I also found that it helped to shoot their close-ups before the master shot. That was a reverse of the usual sequence, which allowed the cameraman to light the whole set first and then adjust for the closer shots. Once, on *Owen Marshall*, the Arthur Hill courtroom drama, the director of photography grew very irritated with my insistence on shooting a child actor's close-ups first. But children are spontaneous and I found that they were often at their best in the very first take.

I had worked with David Janssen on *Richard Diamond* and on an episode of *The Millionaire*, and I had directed *Come Back To Sorrento* for Quinn Martin when he was producing the *Desilu Playhouse*. So it was old home week when I was hired to helm episodes of David's new show *The Fugitive*, which was produced by Quinn. David played Dr. Richard Kimble, an innocent man who was falsely convicted of his wife's murder. On the way to death row, his train derailed and he escaped. He was pursued by a police lieutenant (played by Barry Morse) during each episode, but never caught. Each week he searched for the one-armed man he saw leave the scene of the crime. This was a story idea of Roy Huggins's based on Victor Hugo's classic, *Les Miserables*. The successful series ran for four seasons.

I enjoyed working with Quinn Martin's staff, particularly his editing department, headed by Arthur Fellows. As a director, I could find fault with many film editors but Fellows was always right on. The casting was good, too. The casting director, John Conwell, always recommended good people. Overall, David was a pleasure to work with. And I directed over half a dozen episodes.

On one of them, "Echo of a Nightmare," we were shooting in a mountainous region away from the studio. In the script David had been arrested by a policewoman, played by Shirley Knight. They were handcuffed and the script called for him to use a blowtorch to get away from her. David thought that was ridiculously dangerous and came up with another idea which, out in the wilderness and unable to contact anyone, I went along with. I was severely reprimanded by Martin for changing the script. Up until then, I had been one of Quinn's favorites.

There was another wonderful New York actress, Sandy Dennis, who starred in an episode entitled "The Other Side of the Mountain." There was a scene in which she's climbing a mountain to rescue David and I had a stuntman do the climbing. Sandy didn't understand how it was working, because she had never done much film, so I asked her to come into the editing room so I could show her how it was cut together. Sandy had been very self-conscious about her large rear end. She was thrilled when she saw how the footage came together, because the slim behind of the male stunt double made her look trim. She was a lovely actress who died all too young.

One of my favorite *Fugitive*s was called "The Chinese Sunset." It was written by Leonard Kantor and had a Bogart/Bacall feeling to it. I also liked it because we filmed a block from my apartment, at a small hotel, and my Spanish-style apartment house is visible in the background of the episode. The days we filmed at the hotel allowed me to sleep an extra half hour in the morning and get home earlier, too, instead of having to drive to the studio.

I enjoyed working with James Daly again on the episode "Running Scared." He was a popular television star of *Medical Center* and I had worked with him on my first *Robert Montgomery Presents*. He is of course the father of Tyne and Tim Daly whose paths I crossed when they too became successful performers. The cast supporting him in this episode was particularly wonderful: Joanne Linville, who I had also worked with on *Naked City*, Lin McCarthy, who I had worked with in New York's live television days and was always a pleasure, and Frank Maxwell, another stalwart from live television.

One day we were shooting out in a cemetery in the hills of Los Angeles. We had set up several tombstones with names of characters in the story. It took awhile to get everything set up and just as we were starting to shoot, loud sirens went off. A custodian of the cemetery came over and said there was a fire and that we had to evacuate. My assistant wanted to pack up the crew and move out, but I said, "Let's get the shot first." And we did. Fire or not, the show went on.

The nineteen-sixties were my busiest decade as a director. It was an exciting, groundbreaking period for television. Live television had died out, but I liked shooting on film just as much. The motion picture studios committed fully to television production, and it felt as if the medium was finally taking off. My reputation was good and I was able to direct many of the most acclaimed shows, like *The Twilight Zone*, and to work in every genre without ever becoming "typecast." I directed comedies, like *The Donna Reed Show* at Screen Gems, and a cute sitcom called *Margie* at Twentieth Century-Fox. I directed westerns, like the syndicated, long-running *Death Valley Days*, as well as *Wagon Train*, and *the Virginian*. I did crime shows (*Naked City*), cop shows (*87th Precinct*), courtroom shows (*Perry Mason*), medical shows (*The Nurses*), family shows (*My Three Sons*) and dramatic anthologies (*Alcoa Premiere*). I loved the variety of it, and the feeling of adventure that came with knowing each week would bring new and totally different challenges.

If there was one lot where I spent more time than any other, it was Universal, which produced more television than any of the other majors during this period. Universal Television in the sixties was actually the continuation of Revue Productions, the television production arm of MCA. Headed by Jules Stein and Lew Wasserman, MCA was a powerful talent agency during the fifties, with enough clout to get the unions to go along when it branched into TV production. Like many others in the industry, I was both an MCA client and, when I was directing some of the early shows at Revue, an MCA employee.

MCA's transformation had a dramatic impact on the industry. Outgrowing its small studio space on the former Republic lot in Studio City, MCA purchased the Universal lot a few miles down the road in North Hollywood. The price was $12 million (the studio sold for $6 billion twenty years later). In its new home, MCA/Universal had seventeen film units simultaneously shooting movies and television shows on every corner of the vast North Hollywood lot.

The purchase of Universal caused a great upheaval in the industry. For one thing, it meant that MCA, in order to avoid anti-trust problems with the government, had to dismantle its agency business. Many of MCA's top agents became Universal executives, but others were out on the street, left to find new jobs or start up their own agencies.

Like a lot of MCA clients, I had to find new representation. I went with a smaller agency run by Ronnie Leif (who happened to be Lew Wasserman's son-in-law) and Irving Salkow. (For a television director, agents were necessary for bookings and contracts and follow-throughs. I think they were more booking offices than creative job-finders, but I did always keep working and whether I was the one drumming up trade through my own relationships or whether they did really do some of it, wasn't important.)

87th Precinct was one of my favorite Universal assignments. This police procedural was based on a series of popular novels by Ed McBain, some of which had already been adapted as feature films or live television dramas. Robert Lansing starred as the leader of the cop squad, Detective Steve Carella, and Gena Rowlands appeared occasionally as his hearing-impaired wife. The former head of CBS Television, Hubbell Robinson, was the executive producer in association with MCA, which assigned Boris Kaplan and Winston Miller as staff producers. Directors were hired on a freelance basis, sometimes landing contracts for a certain number of episodes. I was hired to direct a half-dozen.

87th Precinct had to be filmed in six days, sometimes five. It was a tight schedule for an hour-long show. It was set in the fictitious city of Isola (which, like Batman's Gotham City, very much resembled the island of Manhattan) but filmed entirely at Universal Studios. Distant locations were rare for television filming in those early days. Boris and Winston were good producers, and they gave me free rein to shoot it in the live style that I preferred. I could stage long scenes in one take by moving the actors and the camera in and out of close-up when I felt the story needed it, rather than covering the scene and then doing close-ups of everything as some producers demanded. It was a willing cast, and we made some good shows. I remember walking with Winston Miller after we viewed the previous day's filming together. He complimented me on the way I introduced the murderer, with his face reflected in a glass-framed picture of the victim.

I said, "I'm glad you liked that, but I must confess that I borrowed the idea from a movie I saw over the weekend. It was *My Darling Clementine*, John Ford's film about Doc Holiday."

"I know," Winston replied, "I wrote it." Indeed, he had! We worked together often in the future.

Then there were "guest shots" on other series at Universal. Around the same time as *87th Precinct*, I worked on *The Alfred Hitchcock Hour*. I had no contact with Hitchcock, but worked with his producer, Joan Harrison, and the associate producer, Norman Lloyd, who was also a wonderful character actor. Hitch himself directed a few of the half-hour suspense stories and did his delightful introductions, usually filming several in each session. I finished a show for them that another director had dropped out of, and then did an episode of my own. It was not my greatest success. I had a better time working on another Universal anthology, *Alcoa Premiere*.

Alcoa was hosted by Fred Astaire and was something of an attempt to capture the magic of the live dramatic anthologies, even though it was shot on film. I did several of them, all of them featuring some fine actors. One of my episodes starred Richard Kiley and Cloris Leachman. The *Alcoa Premiere* that I remember in particular featured Dana Andrews, the longtime Fox contract player who had starred in Otto Preminger's *Laura*. On *Alcoa* we had two days to rehearse before shooting commenced, an unusual luxury in television. The first day fell on a Friday. We had a table reading, with the writers present. After the rehearsal, they would rewrite. I had asked a girl named Barbara Loden, who I had seen in a movie I liked, *Splendor in the Grass*, to play a featured role in the show. At the first reading she was not very good, and Dana told me I had better replace her. I said, "Let me work with her over the weekend, and then if she doesn't please you, we'll do something about it on Monday."

I invited Barbara to dinner that night and didn't mention the script. I just tried to get to know her. I took her to a party to which I had been invited, and she seemed to have a good time. Monday, at rehearsal, she gave a very good performance. Dana whispered to me, "She's very good, what did you do, fuck her?"

I hadn't. I just relaxed her. I knew Barbara had done very little television, and that she had worked for Elia Kazan (who directed *Splendor*). Kazan worked with people on a personal level, and I knew that held the key — just let her get to know me. As we worked together on that show we were on the same wavelength. Incidentally, Barbara (who died much too young) later married Kazan.

In that same year, Richard Irving, for whom I had done my first television film when he was an executive at Revue, was starting a new series based on *The Virginian*, the popular Owen Wister novel and Gary Cooper feature. James Drury played the Virginian, who had no other name, and the supporting cast (which changed often throughout the years) featured Doug McClure and such stalwarts as Lee J. Cobb and later John McIntyre, John's wife Jeanette Nolan, and at times their real-life son, Tim. *The Virginian* ran on NBC for nine seasons and I think the secret to its longevity was Universal's wise decision to shoot the show in color from the beginning, even though, at the time, most people still owned black-and-white sets.

I did an early episode of this ninety-minute show, which we shot in eight days; as with *87th Precinct* (indeed, with every Universal series), this was a fast schedule, even with the locations confined entirely to the back lot. "The Brazen Bell" guest-starred George C. Scott, who was already a major movie star, as a schoolteacher whose courage (and masculinity) are called into question. At one point, we were shooting a scene where the bad guys have the classroom full of children under gunpoint. The teacher, trying to keep things calm, recites an Oscar Wilde poem to his class. During the run-through, I felt George had overplayed it a bit, and I indicated to him with a hand gesture to take it down a little.

"What kind of direction is that?" he snapped.

I replied calmly. "You're a director, too, George, what would you have said?"

He thought a moment and then said, "Don't let the children see how upset you are."

"That's it, George," I said, and told the assistant to roll it. His words were perhaps what I should have said to him. With Bing Crosby, for instance, I could have just said, "A little softer," and he would have taken it from there. George didn't like me from then on. I think that's why I never got to direct *East Side, West Side*, the acclaimed, New York-based social worker series he made the following season.

East Side, West Side was one of the only New York-based series that I didn't direct during the early sixties. I enjoyed commuting back to my former home, and the material on the few dramas still originating from the East Coast was often gritty and usually good. In 1959, I had been hired to direct several episodes of a half-hour police drama, *Brenner*, which starred James Broderick and Ed Binns. A few years later, I directed E. G. Marshall and Robert Reed in an episode of *The Defenders*, the Emmy-winning legal drama created by Reginald Rose, and one segment of *The Nurses*, with Shirl Conway and Zina Bethune. Both of those shows were produced by Herb Brodkin, a tough, frugal veteran of *Playhouse 90* and other esteemed live dramas.

Brodkin also sent me to London for six weeks, to direct two episodes of an anthology series called *Espionage*. As the title suggested, the show dealt with spies and secret agents each week. But Brodkin was a little too ahead of the curve: the James Bond craze was still a year away, and *Espionage* lasted for only one season.

I loved working in London. A lot of splendid British actors were in the casts of those two shows, and the different customs of the crews were refreshing. Even if we fell behind schedule, tea was served every afternoon. Diane Cilento was in one of my *Espionage*s, and at dinner one night we were joined by her husband, Sean Connery, who was about to become famous as the movies' first James Bond. Connery was very pleasant, but did not reveal the magic that was to come on the screen. Unfortunately his marriage to Diane split up, but they did have a son together, Toby, who is also an actor and quite successful on the British stage.

Although most of the cast and crew of *Espionage* was British, Brodkin sent over a handful of Americans, like myself, to ensure that the production would appeal to a U.S. audience. George Grizzard, my friend from live television, flew over from New York to star in the Diane Cilento episode. Another old friend from New York, Rose Tobias, had taken up permanent residence in London to do the casting for Brodkin there. It was because of Rose that I only did two *Espionage* segments. I cast her husband, an English actor named Maxwell Shaw, in one of the episodes, and Brodkin got mad at me for letting Rose hire her spouse, even though Shaw was fine in the part. That was the end of my stay in England, and of my work on Brodkin's New York series as well.

So I went back to Los Angeles and continued working at Universal on *The Virginian*. One show that I had told my agent I wanted to direct was *Route 66*. I loved the fact that the entire series was shot on distant locations all around the country.

One night in the early sixties, I came home very tired from shooting an episode of Four Star's *Target: The Corrupters*, in which B-movie star Stephen McNally played a newspaper reporter who has infiltrated the mob. At the end of that six-day shoot, I was happily resting in bed at my little house on Norma Place in West Hollywood. Around nine that night the phone rang. It was my agent, Irving Salkow, who said, "I got you a *Route 66!*"

I asked, "When do I get the script?"

"The producer will meet you at the airport in Boston tomorrow morning. You're leaving tonight on the midnight plane."

So I roused myself from sleep and got to the airport. Some hours later, Leonard Freeman, a producer and sometimes writer on *Route 66*, did indeed meet me at the Boston airport. I was immediately ushered into a limousine and given a script to read, as we drove around looking at the various locations within the great, historical landmarks of the Boston area.

"When do we start shooting?" I asked. A director was supposed to have seven days of preparation time for an hour-long television episode.

"Tomorrow," was Leonard's reply. I was soon to realize that late-night phone calls were standard procedure for directors on *Route 66*. Only some days later did I find out that another director had walked off the show the day before I flew into Boston because he couldn't get the rewrites he had requested. Everyone was watching me. I also learned during that time, and fortunately I came through. They liked what I did and I was hired for nine more episodes of *Route 66*, which brought me to Baltimore, Phoenix, Tucson, Dallas, Denver, two in Houston, and Weeki Wachee Springs & Ft. Myers, Florida.

The Baltimore script ("The Mud Nest") had Buzz (George Maharis) thinking he had found his long-lost parents. Lon Chaney Jr. played his supposed father and we had several of Marahis' real brothers and sisters playing Chaney Jr.'s sons and daughters. As it turned out in the scene played in John's Hopkins Hospital, which had Betty Field as Buzz's supposed mother, he sadly found out he was not related.

In Phoenix, Arizona, we had tall, dark motorcyclist Julie Newmar (who I would later work with on *Batman*). She had a very odd personality, but worked well with the boys. She was also a trooper and handled a motorbike very well.

A director got to know the actors better on location as you got to know them socially while staying at these remote hotels. However, sometimes, you had to worry about the actors when staying out on location, particularly those who had a tendency to drink. I remember in Ft. Meyers, Florida, staying up very late with Miriam Hopkins and Ralph Meeker so they would be able to get to bed on time for their very early call.

The producers of *Route 66* seemed to like my work and assigned me to *Naked City* in New York. I remember my first *Naked City* had Nina Foch, the prominent theater and film actress. She had a wonderful taste in clothes and had a fantastic wardrobe that made this chic society lady she was playing come to life.

Naked City was a cop show that focused more on the eccentric street life of New York, where it was filmed in its entirety, than on cops and robbers. Paul Burke played the leading policeman and theater actress Nancy Malone was his neurotic girlfriend. I loved working in the streets of New York and on the locations of *Route 66*. There were so many things happening around you that you always kept getting wonderful, creative ideas.

In Jim Rosen's book on *Naked City* he tells of my adventures in New York's Times Square at 8pm shooting an 11 page scene with Sandy Dennis and Anthony Zerbe in the middle of the theater rush hour, with thousands of people on their busy way to their evening's theater festivities. We had eleven camera moves and would be allowed only one take with these free extras necessary to the drama of the scene. To prevent people from looking in the camera lens we had low lighting on our principals while on another side of the street, as a red herring, we had bright lights and a phony scene staged to protect our real actors from being stared at. Fortunately both actors were proficient on hitting their exact marks in the many moves they had in this very dramatic scene. It worked in the first (and only) take.

Naked City had a great crew with the camera bunch headed by cinematographer Jack Priestly. We worked under unusual circumstances more than once. One evening, it was pouring rain but we stayed out on a rooftop until we got the scene. That episode was *The Highest of Prizes*, which ended up with a surprise ending for all of us. As sometimes happens in television, when we started shooting the episode, Robert Culp's character was written not guilty of murdering his wife and we filmed the scenes accordingly. However, later in rewrites it was decided he was guilty, so we shot the ending that way. It worked, regardless.

Herbert Leonard was the executive producer of *Route 66* and of *Naked City*. He was a terrific producer. As a creative artist, a producer who really knew what he wanted in the content of a show, I put him up there with Fred Coe. Leonard knew how to delegate authority. Though he was based in Hollywood and his shows were shot in distant locations, he was always just a long-distance phone call away. Leonard hired good writers, wonderful crews, and cast splendidly talented actors. I was used to having a major say in casting, but on these two shows the logistics prevented you from getting into that process.

Bert's New York-based casting director, Marion Dougherty, knew the talent pool very well, and discovered some amazing young actors for us to work with. Dustin Hoffman, Gene Hackman & Carroll O'Connor were all actors who Marion cast in *Naked City* when they were just starting out. I became friends with Dustin and Caroll would often invite me to the restaurant he owned.

The scripts on both *Naked City* and *Route 66* were plagued with last-minute rewrites, but on the plus side they were always from incredibly gifted writers: Stirling Silliphant (who created *Route 66* and wrote many of them), Howard Rodman, Abram S. Ginnes and Leonard Freeman.

I learned a lot from Jack Marta, the cinematographer of *Route 66*, like how to pick locations so the sun was on the right side of the street at the right time. When a director had done his homework, as much as possible given the always-late scripts, Jack was on his side. If, on the other hand, the director was vague or unprepared, Marta would get testy. I had to stay on my toes, because we got a lot more film in the can when Jack was happy. In the early days of filmmaking, the directors came from the theater and left a lot of the camera decisions up to the cinematographer. But those of us who came out of live television were very much under the influence of Orson Welles, who was brilliantly creative with his visual images and who was renowned for his productive collaboration with the cinematographer Gregg Toland on *Citizen Kane* and *The Magnificent Ambersons*. We expected to have similar relationships with our cameramen in Hollywood, and although many of them were crusty craftsmen who dated back to the era of hand-cranked cameras, we often prevailed.

Along with *Naked City*, I was able to get back to New York in the mid-sixties to direct episodes of *The Patty Duke Show* and *The Trials of O'Brien*. *The Patty Duke Show* was a comedy vehicle built around the then-fifteen year old actress who had starred on Broadway (and in the subsequent film) as Helen Keller, the blind and deaf girl who learned to talk, in *The Miracle Worker*. It was filmed in New York because the child labor laws there permitted children to work seven hours a day, whereas in California they could only work four hours. Patty had a dual role in her sitcom, as the identical cousins Cathy and Patty Lane, so not only was she on screen nearly all the time, she sometimes had to be photographed *twice* for a single scene.

The Trials of O'Brien was an early "dramedy" starring Peter Falk, years before *Columbo*, as a lawyer with a lot of personal problems. Elaine Stritch had a supporting role as Peter's secretary. At the time she was also understudying the leading role of Martha, the shrewish wife, in *Who's Afraid of Virginia Woolf* on Broadway.

At one point I was directing a scene where Peter comes into Elaine's office on his way into his own. There were a few lines of comic banter between them, and it wasn't playing well in rehearsal. I took Elaine aside and said to her, "I don't know how to tell Elaine Stritch how to play comedy."

She thought for a moment and then said, "Tell her to stop playing *Virginia Woolf*."

I smiled and repeated her advice. We went into the scene and it was perfect. Like George C. Scott on *The Virginian*, she had found her own solution to the problem with only a little prompting from me.

CHAPTER 9

The Bing Crosby Show, Family Affair and *The Love Boat:* Networks Take Control

Since I moved to Los Angeles in 1955, my personal life had changed a great deal. My wife had moved back to New York with our two sons. That was one reason I wanted to work there as much as possible. I rented a small apartment there and was able to visit my sons a lot during my trips to New York.

But by 1964, the number of New York-based television shows had dwindled, and I took a job that put an end to my commuting for a while. This was on *The Bing Crosby Show*, a half-hour musical sitcom that the great singer and movie star had agreed to do on ABC. My agent, George Rosenberg, had been Bing's agent for many years, and he recommended me for the job. At first, I was signed for six shows, we got along very well and my contract was extended to all twenty-eight shows that year.

We filmed *The Bing Crosby Show* at the Desilu Studios. Bing played a father of two daughters and Frank McHugh, the popular character actor of the thirties, was an uncle who lived with them. Beverly Garland was cast as Bing's wife, and Steven Gethers was the producer and primary writer. Bing's regular conductor, John Scott Trotter, handled the music. Each week, Bing did one song which was integrated into the show, and the storyline always included a guest star. Other members of the Crosby family, including Bing's wife Kathryn Grant Crosby and his son Gary, made appearances on the show. Joan Fontaine, who had been Bing's leading lady in the film *The Emperor Waltz*, was the guest star in one of my episodes.

It was a happy time, and I kept the set happy because it wasn't necessary to "direct" Bing playing Bing. One of the things I learned as I worked with him was that he had a tendency to lose his energy as the day progressed. However, when we were working on the musical numbers in each episode, Bing was all there. That gave me the idea of having the rehearsal pianist available at all times, to play in between takes while the lighting crew got ready. The music cheered Bing, and he performed better. The atmosphere on the set was like cocktail party. Other celebrities would drop by sometimes. Even Lucille Ball (who owned the studio) would come on the set to say hello and chat with us once in a while.

Bing, JS, Joan Fontaine and Denis Day.

John Scott Trotter was an important member of the creative staff of that show, and a joy to work with. He had been with Bing for years, and knew just what was workable for him. For the songs, Bing didn't want to pre-record the audio and then have to lip-synch to it when being filmed. Most musical films were done with pre-recording, but we did it live with a piano. Then John Scott would put it together on the dubbing stage, with the orchestra just hired for that session, and synch it to Bing's voice.

Bing was always on time and always very professional, but the perks of stardom were part of his deal on that series. Occasionally, we would use an extra camera to get more coverage without taxing Bing too much. Bing's contract also required us to finish with him by six o'clock every day. It was nice to be able to count on getting home at a reasonable hour. I also enjoyed having a home base instead of going to different locations or soundstages each day. I even had my own office and telephone at Desilu.

The Bing Crosby Show only lasted for one season. It was a pleasant half-hour, although not as successful as Crosby had been in the past. The ratings had not been great, but I'm told the reason the show wasn't picked up was because Bing didn't want to continue. At this point in his life, Bing didn't need the money, or the work. The bursitis in his shoulder caused him pain, and I think he just got bored doing the show. It was a

Bing and Gary Crosby (standing with JS).

shame, because I had a lot of fun working with Bing. When he decided not to keep the series going, Bing sent me a very nice letter, which I have reproduced here.

Before the show was cancelled, Bing's company, which was run for him by Basil Grillo, packaged a pilot for a projected series starring the great Bert Lahr. Elliott Lewis, who had been a famous radio actor and a producer of *The Lucy Show*, produced the pilot, and I was hired to direct.

Bing Crosby
Hollywood

Hillsborough
January 30, 1965

Dear Jim:

I told you on the set, but I wanted to put it in writing - in all my experience, Jim, I've never worked with a nicer fella than you, or a fella more qualified in your job.

Your patience is inexhaustible. I can't recall any time on the set where you ever exhibited any signs of falling apart, blowing up, or taking a walk - and you had many situations where such behavior would have been justifiable. Tremendous control, old boy!

I had a great time just because of the fact that you were at the helm, and in spite of my bursitis problems.

I do hope we can get together on a film sometime - any one of the projects we discussed should be definite possibilities.

As far as the series is concerned, I don't think we made a single episode that we have to be ashamed of or worried about. I just got into that type of thing about five or six years too late.

With all this wild semi-pornographic type of thing that audiences are viewing nowadays, it's not conceivable they're going to have much of an appetite for our gentle, casual stories.

The way the trend is going it's conceivable that

Letter from Bing Crosby.

Bert Lahr was famous as the "Cowardly Lion" from *The Wizard of Oz*, and I had admired him on Broadway for many years. I had heard how difficult Lahr could be, but I found him to be most delightful and cooperative. Lahr played a clumsy ghost who haunted a young couple, and it was a cute show in the vein of fantasy sitcoms like *Bewitched* and *I Dream of Jeannie*, which were popular at the time. However, because Burt was in his mid-seventies and because he was doing a popular commercial for a potato chip company (his famous line was, "I bet you can't eat just one"), *Thompson's Ghost* never sold.

```
            Norman Mailer and Tennessee Williams and fellas of
            that stamp will soon be doing all the writing.

            Well, in any case, we closed on a high point - with
            Pamela Curran on the set, didn't we?

            Hope to see you, Jim, either in New York or on the
            Coast   -

                                        Always your friend,


                                          Bing Crosby

BC:lm

Mr. Jim Sheldon
1302 North Switzer
Los Angeles 69, California
```

After Bing Crosby and Bert Lahr, I worked with another movie legend from the other side of the camera: Walt Disney. I had the pleasure of getting to know him while I was directing five episodes of *The Wonderful World of Color*, these five filmed just before Disney died. There was a series called *Gallagher Goes West*, which was filmed on the Disney lot, and I did two episodes. I also did a three-parter about a seeing-eye dog called *Atta Boy, Kelly*, for which we shot a few scenes in Morristown, New Jersey, the actual training ground of the seeing-eye dogs. Disney might have been a movie mogul, but he was an active producer who got very involved in casting. For one of the leads in the three-part show, Disney preferred an actor whose work I was not familiar with. I went along with the boss, but on the day we arrived in Morristown, this actor had too much to drink on the plane. As we took the bus from the Newark airport, he became more than rambunctious, complaining when the associate producer told him to be on his best behavior since we were representing Walt Disney Productions. He replied, "Fuck Walt Disney." No one heard the remark except a private audience on a bus full of Disney employees. However, after a quick call to Hollywood, the associate producer informed me that the actor would be sent back that night. So, Sean Garrison was replaced by James Olson — who I had wanted in the first place — and the show went on. After a week in Morristown, the company returned to the Disney back lot and we finished the filming there. Arthur Hill and Beau Bridges had the other two leads, but the "stars" were really the several dogs that played Kelly. The dogs were look-alikes and each specialized in a different "trick."

Working at Disney was different from working at any of the other studios. There was more of a gentleness, even in the cafeteria. It was like a college campus watched over by a kindly dean. Even when he was dying, Disney's hospital room overlooked the entrance to his studio and he was able to watch people getting to work on time. After Walt died, his son-in-law, Ron Miller more or less took over the creative side, until many years later when the ABC and Paramount executive Michael Eisner took charge and made it a more profitable operation. I directed a pilot for Ron, a comedic detective show starring Darren McGavin. Darren was very good, but it never sold.

In 1966, *Batman* started and I did a couple of episodes in the first season. This campy, funny take on the Batman comic book briefly became a huge hit for ABC. Adam West starred as Batman and the twenty year-old Burt Ward played his sidekick Robin. Burt lived in Malibu, and he and I got along very well. The studio was annoyed with him because he was not always easy to work with. He came late to the set and made a lot of demands. I decided to chat with him about it and told him how I thought it was unprofessional. Burt just looked at me and said, "Jim, I've got a record contract." However, when the show was over, he found it immensely difficult to continue his career. It was a case of too much, too soon.

In my two *Batman* episodes, Julie Newmar played the villainess, the Catwoman. Julie was having her period while we were shooting, and her condition provoked huge roars from the live tigers that were part of the story. The roaring was so loud that the sound had to be redubbed later. We looped Julie's dialogue in a night session, and afterwards I took her out to Scandia, a popular restaurant on Sunset Boulevard. By the time we got there, the kitchen was closed. I asked Julie if she would like to have a drink. She leaned over, took my hand, and said politely, "No, thanks. I only drink when I'm going to say 'Yes.'"

There were a few series in that period I found silly, but I liked *My Mother, the Car*. It had Anne Sothern's voice playing the talking automobile and Dick VanDyke's brother Jerry played the lead. *O.K. Crackerby* starred Burl Ives as an eccentric millionaire, I think, and the young cast members were Tim Matheson and Brooke Adams. Both of whom went on to busy careers in television. I did one episode of *Julia*, the Diahann Carroll vehicle which broke ground as the first television series to revolve around a modern, independent black woman. Jess Oppenheimer, who had done the *I Love Lucy* show, produced *Julia*. Jess was a fun guy to work for because, try as he did to behave professionally, he couldn't let the director run the set. When we were rehearsing, if Jess didn't like a line reading, you would hear his voice from behind a set onstage someplace, correcting the reading.

Raymond Burr had a hit series with *Perry Mason*, and I enjoyed working with him on that show. In 1967, Universal put together a detective drama called *Ironside* starring Ray. The premise was he was a wheelchair-bound chief of the San Francisco Police Department. I directed nine episodes and enjoyed working with him again. His supporting cast included Don Galloway, Don Mitchell & Barbara Anderson. I found this time instead of scribbling his lines on parts of the set where he was to move to, he had teleprompters for the whole show. He was excellent at using them and his performance was wonderful, despite these odd mechanics. Even the other actors got used to Ray using them. Cy Shermack was the producer for Universal but Ray really ran the ship and he liked me and I liked him. I remember many a night staying up late while he was arguing with Universal V.P. Frank Price about scripts and other details.

When I had run into the problem of trying to shoot on a railroad train on *the Virginian* it was pointed out to me I couldn't have a zoom lens. There were seventeen companies filming at Universal and if they got a zoom lens for one of us, they knew they'd have to get them for everyone. I wanted to use the lens on *Ironside* and Ray had enough clout to secure one for me.

JS and Marlo Thomas.

I had met Marlo Thomas, daughter of Danny, before I was hired to direct her show *That Girl*. I was amazed to find what a hard worker she was. When I arrived on the set she was already in make-up and would emerge two hours later, looking lovely in wonderful clothes designed just for her. Before *That Girl*, I had always worn a jacket and tie to work. One day, Marlo said, "Jimmy, why don't you dress like the rest of us?" From that day on I never wore another tie on set.

I got to do quite a few episodes of *That Girl*, which was produced by Danny Arnold. Danny was pleasant to work for, but the show had a simple format and it didn't tax my creative juices. I remember being glad that I was able to alternate it with the dramatic shows. Later, I worked with Danny again on one of my all-time favorite series, *My World and Welcome To It*, which was based on material by James Thurber. Wikipedia describes the show's premise as follows:

"*My World and Welcome to It* was a US-made half-hour sitcom based on the humor and cartoons of James Thurber. It starred William Windom as John Monroe, a Thurber-like writer and cartoonist who works for a magazine that closely resembles *The New Yorker*, called *The Manhattanite*. Wry, fanciful and curmudgeonly, Monroe observes and comments on life, to the bemusement of his rather sensible wife Ellen (Joan Hotchkis) and intelligent, questioning daughter Lydia (Lisa Gerritsen)."

The show ran on Sundays at seven o'clock, and perhaps was too sophisticated for that time slot. The series won lots of Emmy awards but it only ran one season.

Bill Windom was a joy to work with while Joan Hotchkis was difficult at first. I remember early in the series complimenting her on a scene and suggesting an improvement.

She said "Don't give me any praise, just tell me what you don't like." Her tone was neither warm nor friendly. I thought to myself I'm either going to kiss her or hit her. I decided on the former. We started dating and it turned into a romance and eventually a friendship.

Coincidentally, almost a decade earlier, I had directed a different pilot based on Thurber's stories entitled *Cristobel*, starring Arthur O'Connell. It was equally delightful but that one didn't sell either, but it was aired on *The Goodyear Theatre*. The lovely Georgianne Johnson played O'Connell's wife. Previously, Georiganne had played the love interest of Tony Randall's character on *Mister Peepers*.

In the years since I had directed *The Millionaire* for them, Don Fedderson and his production company had begun to specialize in a very different kind of series: gentle family comedies built around an established movie star. The first and most popular of these was *My Three Sons*, which featured Fred MacMurray (the star of *Double Indemnity* and, later, a number of Disney films). Fred had agreed to do the show only after Fedderson worked out a very agreeable shooting schedule. All of Fred's footage for an entire season would be shot together in thirteen weeks. Then Fred would have the rest of the year off and the crew would shoot everything that did not require his presence — all the scenes and even individual shots involving only the children or Fred's co-star, William Frawley. The Fedderson people brought me onto *My Three Sons* during a crisis. The show's regular director, Jimmy Kern, had died suddenly, after shooting all the secondary material for one season but before any of

MacMurray's scenes had been shot. I finished all of Jimmy's episodes for that year, and got to work with MacMurray, which was a treat.

The Fedderson company liked my work and hired me to direct the pilot film for *Family Affair*. This series was to star Brian Keith as the widowed father of three children. The kids were supposed to be three girls (making the show a sort of distaff *My Three Sons*), but Brian remembered a tal-

William Demarest, Fred MacMurray, Barry Livingston, Stanley Livingston and JS, *My Three Sons*.

ented boy who had appeared with him in the film *The Russians Are Coming, The Russians Are Coming*. Brian suggested that they use this boy, Johnny Whitaker, and the third child became a twin brother of one of the girls.

Family Affair was filmed in the same manner as *My Three Sons*. All the scenes with Brian Keith had to be done in thirteen weeks. The supporting cast included Sebastian Cabot as the family butler, Kathy Garver as the eldest sister, and Anissa Jones as Johnny's twin sister.

Family Affair sold and had a successful, five-year run, but I chose not to continue with the series. During the early filming, I found that Anissa's mother was directing her off camera. I asked her not to. What she was doing ruined the little girl's naturalness. It made Anissa's reactions look canned and cute. Anissa's mother continued doing this until I had to have her banned from the stage. She was not a very cooperative woman — a classic stage mother. After *Family Affair* went off the air, Anissa had a number of personal problems and took her own life when she was only eighteen years old.

Another of the Fedderson single-parent sitcoms was *To Rome With Love*, which featured John Forsythe as a widower who moves to, yes, Rome, with his three daughters. Kay Medford played his sister, who helped with the children. I did thirteen episodes. The show was a cute idea, but it just didn't work. It was never a ratings success and only lasted for two seasons. I suspect that had we actually filmed the show in its entirety in Italy, it might have been a hit. But in those days the studios didn't yet see the value in filming television shows in foreign locations.

During the time I was directing these lighter Don Fedderson shows, I would alternate on heavier dramas. A freelance director's life was filled with variety. I would direct an episode of *The Man from U.N.C.L.E*, an action-adventure drama, and the next week be directing a western like *Gunsmoke* or a police drama like *Felony Squad*. And after a gap of a few years since my last one, I went back to direct more episodes of *The Virginian* at Universal.

One *Virginian* that turned out particularly well was shot on location at Lake Arrowhead. Lois Nettleton and Ricardo Montalban were the guest stars. Ricardo played a French-Canadian fur trapper, and the huge pine trees on the hillside next to Lake Arrowhead doubled convincingly as a Canadian backdrop. That was an overnight location. I had a room in the motel near the crew, and after a day of shooting on location, I was happy to go to bed. One night when I got to my room, the guys on the crew had arranged for a sexy young girl to be waiting there for me. I recognized the girl. She was an extra, who had been hired because the married producer of the show hoped to go to bed with her. Unfortunately for him, his plan had backfired. The girl was more attracted to the director — me. My room was on the first floor and only a few feet from the parking lot, so I reached to pull the blinds down to give us some privacy. But when I pulled the cord, the blinds collapsed in a heap on the floor, leaving us exposed in the window. Just at that moment, the star, Doug McClure, and the producer drove up in front of my room. They had a full view of us in our compromising position. I don't think the producer ever believed me when I tried to explain that I had nothing to go with the girl coming to my room.

One of my favorite episodes of *The Virginian* guest-starred Burgess Meredith and Brandon de Wilde, who had been a tremendously successful child actor on Broadway and in films like *Shane* and was now

JS directing Brenda Scott and Doug McClure in *The Virginian*.

old enough to play a married young rancher. Tyne Daly had her first job in that episode. When she came in to be interviewed for the part, I knew she was the daughter of James Daly, who had been very nice to me when he starred in my first *Robert Montgomery Presents* many years earlier. I asked Tyne who she had studied with, and she mentioned Sanford Meisner. She seemed right for the part and I cast her. Twenty years later, when she was starring on Broadway in the revival of *Gypsy*, she won a Tony. I saw her at an affair and when I offered my congratulations, she said, "Thank you, and I owe you an apology. Twenty years ago I lied to you when I had said I had studied with Meisner, but I heard you liked actors who studied with Meisner."

I said, "That's not why you got the part. You got the part because your father was so nice to me when I did my first dramatic show." I worked with Tyne again on *Cagney & Lacey*, in an episode that introduced Sharon Gless to replace Loretta Swit, the original co-star of the two-hour pilot film. I worked with her father again, too, in an episode of *The Fugitive*.

In 1969, I directed my first made-for-television film, an ABC movie called *Gidget Grows Up*. During the next decade, movies created originally for television would take up a substantial amount of the networks' schedules, and would attract many of the most talented people who worked in the medium. I attribute the popularity of the TV movie to two things. First, the networks were running out of old movies to rerun. Second, they saw the television film as a budget-conscious showcase for actors who were appearing in their series, and therefore a way to cross-promote both projects. This idea was the invention, in particular, of Barry Diller, then the head of programming at ABC, where the "Movie of the Week" first began to achieve both popular and critical success.

Gidget Grows Up was a third attempt to rekindle the surfer-girl franchise that had been a series of films at Columbia, and a short-lived series starring Sally Field. Instead of trying to lure back Sandra Dee, the first of the Gidgets, the studio chose Karen Valentine, an unknown actress who was to be a regular in the forthcoming series *Room 222*. I also didn't get the leading man I wanted. Instead, I was given Edward Mulhare, the star of the sitcom *The Ghost and Mrs. Muir*, which was moving from NBC to ABC that season.

On *Gidget Grows Up*, we shot for one week in New York City, and then for another two weeks back in Los Angeles, on a soundstage at Columbia Pictures. In those days, we couldn't get cooperation with the New York police. *Gidget* had a scene with a firecracker going off, and I saved it for last and suggested we pack everything up just before shooting it. It was a wise decision. On *Naked City*, I had learned that in New York it was better to get the shot and run rather than ask permission beforehand. It was still the same in 1969. Today, it's totally different; New York City has a department to help film crews, and it brings a lot of money to the city!

Karen Valentine had some temper tantrums during that first week, but as we progressed and the film went well she and I became good friends. Soon I would be directing Karen on *Room 222*, and I also went to her first wedding. When her charming first husband knelt at the altar, we could all see that someone had painted the word "Help!" on the soles of his shoes.

Karen's big final scene in the movie occurred in front of Tiffany's famous jewelry store at night. Naturally, it was scheduled for our first week in New York, but shooting this final scene so early in the schedule worried me. I felt it would go much better after Karen and her leading man, Paul Petersen (who I had directed on *The Donna Reed Show*, when he was still a boy), had worked together for a while. I filmed the introductions to the scene on the actual location, in front of Tiffany's at Fifth Avenue and 57th Street, but I saved the close-ups to do on stage, two weeks later, against a rear screen projection. By that time, I reasoned, Karen and Paul, who she was to marry in this episode, would have gotten to know each other better and would play off each other more naturally. To do this I needed a background film plate of the location, and I shot it without asking permission. Seymour Friedman, the efficient production manager at Columbia Pictures, got annoyed with me. But I still think I made the right decision, and I think deep down Seymour knew it was right, too. The scene played much better than if we had shot it before Karen, a novice, had had time to fully immerse herself in the part.

Politics are an unavoidable part of the television industry, and *Gidget Grows Up* was a good example of a show on which I ran afoul of them. Renee Valente was a casting director at Columbia Pictures, and also the liaison between the studio and Barry Diller, the ABC executive in charge of this project. She was a wheeler-dealer. When we were conferring over the casting of *Gidget Grows Up*, I voiced objections to some actors who I thought would be miscast if they were chosen. But all of them were regulars on current or upcoming ABC series, and I didn't realize the extent to which Diller was invested in using them. I think Renee agreed with me, but for political reasons she sided with Diller. She also told Diller, over the phone and with me in the room, that I didn't think one of his actors was right for the part. That didn't endear me to Diller and I never got to work for him again. I continued to direct episodic television for ABC, but I think I might have been able to do more movies of the week had that one conversation not taken place. I did maintain a friendship with Renee, who spent the Fourth of July with our kids at my Malibu beach pad one year. She became a producer and did some good work, but I never worked for her. Renee once told me that she wanted me for a job, but that the network wanted someone else. It was probably true. That was how the politics of the business work. Some people loved me, and some obviously didn't.

One summer, I directed nine episodes of *Room 222*, a Twentieth Century-Fox production. It was produced by Bill D'Angelo, the Associate Producer of *Batman*. The Executive Producer was Gene Reynolds, a former child star, who I had worked with on *Robert Montgomery*. *Room 222* was a fun show, set in a high school, with a young, enthusiastic cast. What I remember most about it was that my son, James Jr., worked as a regular extra in the classroom that summer and was on the set almost every day. James saved up his money, took the next year off from college, and traveled around the world. I met up with him in Morocco in February, and we went to Crete together in May. Most years, production on a television season finished by February and didn't start again until June or July. I had time to see the world during those hiatuses, and I took advantage of it, particularly when my sons were away at school.

My brother had settled in London, and my father had gone to live with him. So London was a good place to start when I took off on one of my trips, not only to visit family but also to see plays and continue broadening my knowledge of young talent.

On one of those London trips, I became part of a venture that seemed as if it would launch me as a feature film director. My brother worked for a very successful international businessman, and through him I got an appointment to pitch an idea I'd been thinking over for a while. I had observed how Don Fedderson had corralled motion picture stars who might not otherwise work in television by separating out all their scenes and condensing their schedule to a guaranteed thirteen weeks. That left the actors free to continue their movie careers without getting tied down to a series for eight months out of the year. I had figured out a way to adapt this plan to motion picture production, and now I hoped that my brother's employer, Bernie Cornfeld, might finance it.

A morning meeting with Cornfeld turned into a week-long journey around the continent. Cornfeld was then the head of a successful international mutual fund headquartering in Geneva, but he was also starting a "leisure world" set-up in several countries. In addition to selling homes, he wanted his developments to have their own clothing line, for which he had lined up the designer Oleg Cassini, and their own theatres, to show films which Cornfeld would produce. Even before I arrived on the scene, he had been excited about getting into show business. He had been in touch with the William Morris Agency, and had gotten the actor Laurence Harvey involved.

Cornfeld asked me if I would like to work for him. This wasn't what I had come for, exactly, but it sounded intriguing. It was at a quiet time in television production in Los Angeles, the end of the season, and staying in London would be a welcome change. Cornfeld paid me a comfortable salary and I lived near him. We flew to his headquarters in Geneva, to Rome, to Paris, all on his private jet. All of a sudden, everybody was calling me. I was the big shot. My job was to line up several motion picture properties, so that we would have a production board similar to the one I had come to pitch. It would be a season of feature films, to be filmed contiguously. One of the properties was a book called *Bird*. I really thought I had arrived.

Then the bottom dropped out. Cornfeld had spent so much time on our film project he had not noticed as some of his partners in the overseas investment services bilked the company. All of a sudden, our ambitious moviemaking plans fell apart. I went back to Los Angeles and started to renew my television contacts. I don't feel this was a setback in my career, just something that could have been wonderful but turned out to be nothing.

CHAPTER 10

Sanford & Son, M*A*S*H and The Love Boat: Ratings Soar But the Fun Is Gone

I returned home from London in 1971, disappointed that my new career as a movie mogul was not to be but ready to go back to work. My first show of the new season was a new hour-long legal drama called *Owen Marshall, Counselor at Law*. Jon Epstein produced the series for Universal, and the stars were Arthur Hill and Lee Majors. Arthur had played one of the leads in my three-part Disney movie, *Atta Girl, Kelly*, and had been a star on Broadway in *Who's Afraid of Virginia Woolf* and *The Matchmaker*. I had known Lee Majors when he was just starting to act and his name was still Lee Yeary.

One of my favorite agents in Los Angeles was a man I met through my friend Jane Deacy, the agent in New York to whom I had first introduced James Dean. Jane's West Coast representative was a man named Dick Clayton, who had handled James Dean for her during Dean's brief time in Hollywood. Dick was never my agent, but he always recommended me for jobs when he could. He also recommended actors to me, and I always felt comfortable hiring anyone he endorsed. Dick had steered me to Burt Reynolds, who I cast on *Route 66* long before he became famous, and to Lee Majors. While I was directing a show called *Apple's Way*, Dick introduced me to Farrah Fawcett. There was a script in which Vince Van Patten's character falls in love with an "older" woman with whom he plays tennis. Farrah hadn't acted much before, but was physically perfect and a good tennis player. That episode came off well and, unbeknownst to me at the time, Farrah and Vince became very close friends.

I directed thirteen *Owen Marshall* episodes in the next three seasons. Unlike many of the line producers at Universal, Jon was a gentleman and was very considerate of his directors. Most of the time I was able to cast the actors I felt were right for the part. Once, however, a studio executive asked Jon to use his wife in an *Owen Marshall*. I had seen the role played differently, but I did what I was told. That kind of nepotism wasn't common in Hollywood, but it did happen. Another casting difficulty I recall involved an unknown young actor who was cast in one of my episodes On the first day I found his delivery to be very slow, and decided it would be prudent to rehearse with him before the next day's shooting. We went over his scenes, alone, several times. This actor improved, and he appreciated my extra effort. His name was Mark Hamill, and a few years later he played Luke Skywalker in *Star Wars*.

On *Owen Marshall*, I had an argument with the cameraman about shooting a close-up before the master shot. It was a big, emotional courtroom scene, and on the witness stand was a ten year-old girl. From my experience with child actors, I didn't want her to have her big moment in a long shot. I wanted the freshness of the performance up close. I won the point. The little girl was so much better in the first take than in the master shot that everyone on the set knew I was right. That cameraman, Harkness Smith, did good work, but he was testy. I remember him complaining to me about a director who had done an *Owen Marshall* in between two of my episodes. There was a scene involving a high school football game and the director wanted to put the camera on the ground and shoot up at the sky from the center of the football players' huddle. Smith shot it that way, but he hated it. That director's episode was very successful. He had already done a very successful TV-movie for Universal, about a homicidal tractor trailer truck, and soon he would be assigned to direct *Jaws*. Of course, it was Steven Spielberg.

At Paramount, I directed segments of *Love, American Style*. The producers were two writers whose scripts I had directed on *That Girl*, Saul Turtletaub and Bernie Orenstein. *Love, American Style* was a forerunner of *The Love Boat*. It had several stories in each half-hour episode, all having to do with romance in some way. There were no series regulars and no big names among the guest stars, but the scripts were funny and short and sweet. The titles give you an indication: "Love and the Mind Reader," "Love and the Mail," "Love and the Cozy Comrades." Often the casts of these vignettes were made up of Broadway actors who knew their way around comedy, like Warren Berlinger, Jo Anne Worley, Larry Storch, Alice Ghostley, and Rich Little. One actor I worked with on *Love, American Style* was Joyce Van Patten. She and her brother Dick had started as child actors. When they were still teenagers, I had dated their mother who worked as an agent. I worked with Joyce many times in serious dramatic roles.

Saul and Bernie went on to produce *Sanford and Son*, and hired me for six of those. This was 1975, and *Sanford and Son* was one of the first successful comedies about African American life, with an all-black cast. *Sanford and Son* was a popular situation comedy and like many sitcoms it was filmed before a live studio audience. It was rehearsed in advance, usually for several days, and then rehearsed with the cameras. There was usually a dress rehearsal without an audience, and then the audience was let in. Usually there were several hundred people. Either the star of the show or a person adept at warming up a crowd would explain what was to happen and encourage them to laugh at the jokes. (This could be enlarged later with a laugh track editorially). Usually the show would run through from start to finish. If something went wrong or didn't play well, technically or dramatically, the audience would be asked to stay and the scene would be done again. On occasion, it might be done again without the audience.

I was happy to be a part of it, and although they treated me like "that white boy" I got along very well with most of the actors. Redd Foxx, who played Fred Sanford, was a lot of fun to work with, although he was a bit outrageous in getting the audience to respond. He would resort to any trick, including unzipping his fly, but he definitely knew how to get his laugh.

Lorimar Productions had started up with *The Waltons*, a Depression-era family drama that was a major hit in 1972. Eventually I directed a couple of the last episodes of *The Waltons* in 1981, but I first worked for Lorimar on some of the more short-lived series they sold in the wake of *The Waltons*' success. One of them was *Doc Elliott*, with James Franciscus in the title role of a country doctor. Neva Patterson was a regular on the series, playing Doc Elliot's nurse. We shot a lot of the show on location in a mountain village not far from Los Angeles.

Having worked with him before, I knew that Jim Franciscus liked to get his close-up coverage done early, and on the first day of work I set the staging so that the first set-up tightened in on Jim and we covered his dialogue all in one. Neva Patterson remained off camera during Jim's big speech. After Jim's close-up was finished, we set up for Neva's reverse shot. As the cameraman reset the lights, I whispered something in Neva's ear. She was terribly good during the take, much richer and fuller than she had been off-stage during Jim's close-up.

Later, Jim asked me what I had whispered to Neva. I'd only spoken to her for two seconds, he said.

"It wasn't two seconds," I replied, "it was thirty years." Neva and I used to be very close friends and I knew just what to tell her. She had been the girl in the skimpy costume who held up the title cards between acts on the first *We, the People* telecast. We had dated, and had a lot of fun together, in those New York days. By the time of *Doc Elliot*, she had moved to Los Angeles and married the writer James Lee, but she was still as beautiful as ever.

Another show I did for Lorimar was *Apple's Way*. It was a family show, and one of the sons was played by sixteen year-old Vincent Van Patten, who later became a pro tennis player. Vincent was one of Dick Van Patten's sons, and on the set one day he said "You used to date my grandmother!"

Meanwhile, at Twentieth Century-Fox, much of the studio's lot in West Los Angeles had been razed since I first came to Hollywood. The fiasco of *Cleopatra* had forced Fox to sell its back lot to Alcoa, and they used the land to build Century City, a modern apartment complex and shopping center. But Fox still had a viable television department, and one of its big projects for 1972 was a television series version of *The King and I*, the hugely successful 1956 musical film. Fox's coup was getting the original king, Yul Brynner, to reprise his role for the TV series. Samantha Eggar stepped into the role originated by Deborah Kerr.

I loved this show, which was called *Anna and the King*. The costumes and sets from the original feature film had been pulled out of Fox's storage, and therefore the series looked much more opulent than most half-hour comedies. And it was also a pleasure to sit on an air-conditioned set during the hot summer. But after two episodes where I delighted in working with King Yul, the studio assigned me to its other new show of the season, which filmed part-time out in the hot, dusty Malibu Hills, with a cast of army medics in dirty green fatigues. This one was based on another, more recent movie from the Fox catalog: *M*A*S*H*.

Now I substituted the friendly atmosphere of the Brynner company for the somewhat more contentious personalities of Alan Alda, Wayne Rogers, McLean Stevenson and others. The scripts, written or supervised by Larry Gelbart, were great. However, there were technical challenges related to shooting inside the tents in which all the characters lived and worked. Lighting the inside of the tents took more time, so we couldn't always get the film coverage we wanted. There were also serious problems involving actors upstaging one another. The rivalry between Alan Alda and Wayne Rogers led to Wayne leaving the show and being replaced by Mike Farrell. By this time, the public had warmed to Alan's character and Mike (unlike Wayne) didn't mind playing second fiddle. Being a family man, he was happy to be on such a successful show. I didn't find it a particularly joyous atmosphere to work in. Alan was very professional but he was always fighting to stay center stage. In a situation where so many guys are competing to be the star, Alan dominated and irritated some of the other actors. Stevenson was unhappy with the way his role was going and, when offered his own series, left in favor of that. Stevenson asked me to direct the pilot of his new show, *The McLean Stevenson Show*, which I did, but it never went anywhere. Of the girls, the most successful was Loretta Swit, she reappeared on *M*A*S*H* often during its run. Loretta had a natural comedy quality and was very professional and not disturbed outwardly about all the politics between the men. As I recall Gary Burghoff was in his own world too and his character, Radar, was always very effective. *M*A*S*H* ran eleven years, and *Anna and the King* never finished its first season.

Gene Reynolds was the executive producer on *M*A*S*H*, and he thought I shot too many close-ups on my one episode from the first season. I was not hired to direct any more that season, however, the next year, after Farrell had replaced Rogers, I returned for one more episode. I wish I had played the politics of that situation more successfully and done more on *M*A*S*H*, if only because I still get a fee whenever my two episodes are rerun. So far, they have been repeated at least a hundred times.

After *Owen Marshall* went off the air, Jon Epstein had moved on to produce *McMillan & Wife*, a series of two-hour television mysteries starring Rock Hudson. Jon hired me to direct an episode in 1974. In the show, Hudson played a police detective in San Francisco and Susan St. James played his wife, an amateur sleuth. Nancy Walker, the Broadway comedienne and soon to be one of the stars of *Rhoda*, was their housekeeper. Although the setting was San Francisco, *McMillan and Wife* was shot entirely on Los Angeles locations and on a stage at Universal Studios. The series was a popular comedy/mystery on NBC and somewhat like the Nick and Nora Charles films in its tone. I was pleased to get the assignment.

During my first day on the set, I tried to make friends with the star. Rock Hudson was very imposing in person. "I was a friend of James Dean," I said, since Rock had made the movie *Giant* with Jimmy.

Instead of the friendly reply I was expecting, all Rock said was, "That prick."

I realized I was on the wrong track and left the subject alone, but fortunately the episode went well and I was hired to direct *McMillan and Wife* again. Once I had gotten more comfortable with Rock, who I was now calling Roy, I asked him why he didn't like Jimmy. I added I had never seen *Giant* because Jimmy was a friend of mine and I was too upset by his death to see it when it came out.

Rock invited me to come to his house for dinner and to watch *Giant* in his private screening room. I saw in the picture Rock and Jimmy played rivals. Rock and I discussed how difficult Jimmy was for him to work with. "Liz liked him," Rock said, meaning Elizabeth Taylor, "but he was really unpleasant to me."

I knew that Jimmy's method of working meant that he played his part 24/7. I explained to Rock that Jimmy had stayed in character the whole time they were making *Giant*, and that the hostility Rock experienced came from the character of Jett Rink, not from Jimmy himself. By the seventies, I think Rock had run into enough method actors to understand where Jimmy was coming from. I felt I had done a friend a favor.

Another sophisticated mystery series at Universal that I enjoyed very much was an hour drama based on the adventures of Ellery Queen. In this incarnation, the popular literary detective was played by former MGM star Jim Hutton. His co-star, playing Ellery's father, was Broadway actor David Wayne. The series also had some terrific guest stars. One of my episodes featured both Betty White and Eve Arden.

During the filming of one of my *Ellery Queen*s, Jim Hutton' son, Tim, came to the set. He was fifteen at the time, and had not seen much of his father since his parents' divorce. I was able to smooth things over between them during some tense moments. Sadly, Jim died very young, only a few years after *Ellery Queen*'s one season on the air. Timothy, his son, grew into a fine actor in his own right, and is still working today.

Around the same time, I directed a lawyer show called *Petrocelli*. Barry Newman played the lead, and Albert Salmi starred opposite him as the local sheriff. We filmed the whole show on location, in Tucson, Arizona, and I was delighted to find that I had pretty much the same crew that had worked on the *Route 66* I had directed in Tucson a decade earlier. The show was well-received but it wasn't a smash, and it only ran two seasons.

Also in the mid-seventies, Bill D'Angelo, for whom I had worked on *Batman* and *Room 222*, was producing a new half-hour comedy at Warner Brothers starring Linda Lavin, who at that time was known mainly for her stage work. It was based on the successful film *Alice Doesn't Live Here Anymore*, which was written by Bob Getchell and directed by Martin Scorsese. The series was called simply *Alice*, and started shooting in the summer of 1976.

The original plan was to do *Alice* on tape before a live audience. I found that, although Linda was a good actress, she tended to perform for the audience and came across as a little broad in the camera close-up. I suggested to the producers that it would work better to do it without an audience, especially since they were adding a sweetened laugh track anyway. I also recommended the writing team who had written so much great material for Lucille Ball. Madelyn Pugh Davis and Bob Carroll, Jr. were hired to write for the series. I directed several episodes during that first season, and *Alice* ran for a number of years.

Another comedy that I rather liked was *Bridget Loves Bernie*, which was loosely derived from the old play *Abie's Irish Rose*. Meredith Baxter and David Birney, who would soon marry in real life, starred in the title roles as young newlyweds in an interfaith marriage. He was a nice Jewish boy and she was a nice Irish-Catholic girl, but the premise was still mildly controversial. Much of the action took place in the Jewish delicatessen owned by Bernie's parents. I enjoyed the show, but it didn't go past one season.

Bridget Loves Bernie was produced by Douglas Cramer, for whom I later worked on *Love Boat*. We clashed during our first meeting. In one of my *Bridget Loves Bernie* segments, I thought that David Birney's performance was a little bit slow. I told David I would like to take it once more and at a faster tempo. He started to argue with me, saying he felt the pace was right. I said, "I will print the first one, but I would also like to try it faster. If you come in to see the dailies tomorrow, and say that the faster one is not better, I'll use the other take." I always thought the diplomatic approach was an easier way to get along with a star. David came with me to the dailies, and he agreed with me. That put our relationship on a good footing and from then on I never had any disagreements with him. The down side was that Cramer did not like his actors to see the dailies, a fact of which I was unaware. I was called on the carpet, but when I explained to Cramer why I did it, he understood. I worked with him several times in the future, and he even invited me to his very elegant Christmas dinners.

When I worked with Cramer again on *Love Boat*, he had joined forces with Aaron Spelling. Both of them were well connected with the network brass, and in the late seventies they were producing several hit shows including *Love Boat*, *Dynasty*, and *Family*. *Love Boat* was a tricky situation. Each hour-long script included three or four different stories, which were filmed separately but interwoven into a single episode. This meant that, at times, segments by different directors were combined within a single episode.

I directed several *Love Boat*s, and the best part of that experience was the roster of comedy stars who appeared on the show. Milton Berle, Pearl Bailey and Phyllis Diller all worked in my episodes. Doug knew I was a ballet fan, and hired me to direct an episode featuring two ballet stars, John Meehan of the American Ballet Theater and Starr Danias of the Joffrey Ballet. The storyline had the dancing couple traveling on the Love Boat as performers, while the young man was concealing a serious illness from his partner. For John and Starr's shipboard performance, we did selections from the classic *Swan Lake* ballet.

Overall, I found that *Love Boat* offered less directorial control than I was accustomed to. When I was told by the film editor that Spelling wanted close-ups of every scene, and he would decide what was used, I did as requested but lost my creative enthusiasm. Based on the residual checks that still come in, I wish that I had anticipated the popularity of *Love Boat* and stayed with the show longer.

There was less interference from Spelling when I directed a couple episodes of *Family*, a critically acclaimed domestic drama that also had Mike Nichols as an executive producer (although I never met him). It was a very well-written show that starred Sada Thompson and James Broderick (Matthew's father), along with a very attractive younger cast including Meredith Baxter (from *Bridget Loves Bernie*) and Kristy McNichol. I had worked with Broderick in the past on his show *Brenner* and on *The Fugitive*, and Sada Thompson was one of Broadway's unique actresses. The scripts under the influence of Broadway playwright Jay Presson Allen (*The Prime of Miss Jean Brodie*) were quite good.

The seventies were the period during which the "Movie of the Week" became very popular. I was so busy with my episodic assignments that I only did a few of them. One I particularly enjoyed was called *With This Ring*. It was about wedding caterers and combined several different stories to showcase various television stars who were popular at the time: Tony Bill, Joyce DeWitt, John Forsythe, Dick Van Patten, Betty White, Mary Crosby, and others. We filmed *With This Ring* at Paramount and at various locations in Los Angeles, including lobbies and rooms of the Bonaventure Hotel. This very modern hotel was photogenic but not easy to light. One particularly long, difficult scene had to be filmed at night in the lobby. It required some intricate camera moves, and the actors were required to hit some very precise marks. The studio was going to pull the plug on me at 9:30, and we weren't ready to start the take on this scene until 9:25. There was a lot of tension in the air. Fortunately — because it was the only take I was going to get — the scene worked on the first take. I shouted "Cut! Print! Wrap!" One of the actors, a well-built, muscular young man named Scott Hylands, started coming towards me. I thought, "He's angry about what I've put the actors through, and he's going to hit me." When Scott reached me, he said, "You have grace under pressure." I was pleased to find that the physically imposing actor, a veteran of the American Conservatory Theater, was paying me a compliment.

Some of the other shows I worked on during my free weeks were not as gratifying. These were forgettable ventures like *Monster Squad* and *McDuff, the Talking Dog* — kids' shows, really. They did not have very

Pearl Bailey and JS, *Love Boat*, 1982.

long-lasting runs, but they were surprisingly fun to do and they helped pay the bills.

The last things I directed during the seventies were a couple of episodes of *Knots Landing*, a new series that spun off some of the characters from the successful prime-time soap opera *Dallas*. The cast included Michele Lee, Joan Van Ark, Ted Shackelford, and Donna Mills. Larry Hagman had become a big star again as J.R., the villain of *Dallas*, and to help launch the new show he made a guest appearance on *Knots Landing*. The series was produced at Lorimar by the creator of *Dallas*, David Jacobs. I enjoyed getting it started, even though I didn't enjoy the creator. I think that by the time *Knots Landing* began, the success of *Dallas* had gone to his head. I find writers are the most valuable commodity. Many times executives, to keep them happy, make them producers. It's been my experience that producers who worked their way up the production ladder are more secure in working with the director. Many writers who shot straight up to being a producer on a series often were less tactful and less inclusive with their directors. They think they can do everything themselves and don't include the director in important aspects of production, especially the casting.

Except for the producer's brother-in-law in one of the leads, it had a marvelous cast and a wonderful look. It was a nighttime soap opera with interesting characters in the same mold as *Dallas*.

Hagman and I continued our friendship from the *West Point Story* days, particularly when I lived near him on the beach in Malibu. He handled his success very well and had a very happy and long-lasting marriage. In viewing the show again many years later, I was surprised how sexual the storyline was.

Unfortunately, I had more than a few experiences where my stint on a series was soured by a conflict with someone in power there. It happened on *Switch*, for instance, which was a caper series at Universal produced by my friend Jon Epstein. The stars were Robert Wagner and Eddie Albert. I knew Eddie from our live television days, and we got along fine. But Robert Wagner was a problem. More than anyone, he played the movie star. His wife, Natalie Wood, would drop by the set, and he often kept the company waiting. I confronted Wagner about this problem, and he replied that he had a life besides just doing a television show. I didn't like his attitude toward the work, and from then on he didn't like me, either. A few years later, I was hired to direct an episode of *Hart to Hart*, Wagner's subsequent series. He had me removed from that show. I didn't always make friends and influence people.

CHAPTER 11

Cagney & Lacey, The Dukes of Hazzard and *The Equalizer:* Lots of Cops, Lots of Robbers

The silver lining of the cloud that was *Switch* was with Sharon Gless, a young contract player at Universal who had a supporting role as a secretary on the show. Sharon and I got along very well on *Switch* and then again, a few years later, when she became one of the stars of *Cagney & Lacey*. Sharon was the third actress to play the character of Chris Cagney, following Loretta Swit (in the pilot) and Meg Foster (who had been fired by CBS after six episodes). I was hired to direct Sharon's first episode.

But *Cagney & Lacey* turned into another unpleasant story. It should have been a good experience; after all, I liked Sharon, I had worked with Tyne Daly (who played the other policewoman, Lacey) before, and I got along well with the creator and executive producer, Barney Rosenzweig, who was also my neighbor. But CBS had assigned two line producers to the show, and they were not up to the job. They were knowledgeable enough about scripts, but not experienced in the area of casting. The script for my episode centered around an elderly man, and the two line producers insisted on hiring an actor I had never even heard of whose headshot they saw in a casting book, and who seemed inadequate for the part. I went to Barney and asked him to intercede, but was disappointed when he said, "Jim, go along with it. The network stuck me with them, and I'm trying to get them fired."

I went ahead with the producers' casting, since I didn't have much choice and assumed I could get a performance out of anybody. Well, I couldn't. The elderly actor was terrible. Barney had been willing to let the producing pair fail conspicuously in order to get rid of them, and his plan worked: they were fired. Unfortunately, I was never hired to direct *Cagney & Lacey* again. In a system where the director is a freelancer and everyone else is on staff, it's easy to make the director the scapegoat. At least I remained friends with Sharon, having helped her with the difficult task of replacing another actress on a production that was messy and disorganized. She later married the executive producer Barney Rosenzweig but I always got a hug anytime I'd run into her.

From there I moved on to a couple episodes of *The Waltons*, and then to a show featuring the original star of that show, Michael Learned. Michael played the title character in *Nurse*, a medical drama which co-starred Robert Reed (who I had directed in *The Defenders*). The series was shot in New York, where I loved to work, and I directed every other episode for several months. CBS gave me a generous expense account, and it was a pleasant way to end the year. However, the scripts for *Nurse* were sub par and, ultimately, it was a routine hospital show. It only lasted for one season.

I returned to Los Angeles at my agents' request, and was assigned to do an episode of an action-adventure show *240-Robert*, which was about a special search and rescue squad of the Los Angeles County Sheriff's Department. The creator and executive producer of the show was Rick Rosner, who had created the hit cop show *CHiPs*. Like most episodes of the series, my first *240-Robert* featured an elaborate action sequence with a lot of stunts. It started with a chase scene down a mountain as the sheriffs tried to catch a runaway car. In addition to the main characters pursuing the car in a jeep, there was also a helicopter overhead. I lucked into very good weather and finished the first day's chase on schedule.

The episode had another location day, involving a bank robbery that we staged in a practical location in Anaheim. The script called for one of the characters to fire his gun at the ceiling and shoot down the chandelier. However, the bank in which we were filming did not have a chandelier. I talked to Rick Rosner about the problem, and he said that he would come to the set and rewrite the scene. When the rewrite was done, I didn't like what Rick had written, but I knew that the cast and crew thought highly of him and went ahead with the changes. Halfway through the shooting, I decided the scene was so bad I had to call "Cut!" I said, "Rick, that just isn't very good."

Everyone in the unit was surprised and a little concerned after I challenged Rick openly. He asked, "How would you do it?" He had put me on the spot but just at that moment I got an idea of how to do the scene. It worked, and that episode became the best they had done up to that time. The bank robbery scene made me look good, and I came back to direct several more episodes.

One reason I didn't share the awe in which the *240-Robert* crew seemed to hold Rosner was that I was still angry with him about an incident that occurred during pre-production. I was in New York when I was booked for the show, and my agent told me it started preparation on the 24th of December. I wanted to spend the holidays with my children, and my agent suggested that if I called Rosner he would be sure to agree to let me stay in New York until after Christmas. But when I spoke to Rick, he refused. He said, "Everybody tells me how good you are, but I don't know you. I'd like to have you here for the preparation. You're getting paid."

So I went to Los Angeles as required on December 24th and there was no script. I spent a lonely Christmas away from my family and unable to do any prep work on my *240-Robert* assignment. On December 26th, there was still no script, and there continued to be no script until December 29th, two days before we began shooting. I had to rush through the process of casting the guest actors and choosing the locations. By that point, I didn't like working for Rick very much. However, after the success of my first *240-Robert*, he recommended me to several other producers who kept me busy for the next few years. I also worked for Rick again on his next series, *Lottery*.

Another difficult but interesting producer I worked for in the eighties was Irwin Allen, whose claim to fame was a series of popular, all-star movies about epic manmade or natural disasters. Allen was starting a television series called *Code Red*, in which the disasters would consist of big fires each week. Lorne Greene and Andrew Stevens starred in the show as father-and-son firefighters. The series was interesting for me mainly because of all the technical elements I had not worked with before: stunts and "pyro" effects related to the fires that provided the action in each episode. At the end of every segment, one of the actors delivered a lecture about some aspect of fire prevention or safety directly to the audience. I had affection for these short public service messages, because they reminded me of the *Crimes of Carelessness* radio program that I had produced more than thirty years earlier.

Irwin Allen was a hands-on producer. He liked to show up on the set in the middle of a scene and yell, "More smoke! More smoke!" Of course, he wouldn't know where the cameras were positioned, and his extra smoke would get in the way and interfere with whatever shot I had planned. In most cases, it would have been highly obnoxious for a producer to stride onto set and override the director. But the crew found Irwin amusing, and so did I. *Code Red* only ran for a year, probably because NBC scheduled it at 7pm on Sundays. It might have been more successful at a more adult hour.

One of the producers to whom Rick Rosner had recommended me was David Gerber, who had made a name for himself on the series *Police*

Story and *Police Woman*. David hired me to direct an episode of his new series, *McClain's Law*. The show had Jim Arness, who I had directed on *Gunsmoke*, as an ex-cop who, in the pilot, came out of retirement to solve his best friend's murder. McClain decided to stay on the force and mentor a group of younger police officers, and thus the series continued (although for less than a season). Gerber was very complimentary after

Kim Cattrall and JS, *The Gossip Columnist*.

my first *McClain's Law*, and told me that regular actors on the show were better in my episode than they had been with other directors. He asked me what my secret was. I didn't know, exactly, and told David that. He didn't believe me; he felt I was keeping something from him.

When I did the next episode, I asked one of the younger actors what I did that was different than other directors. He said, "You make us feel like you *like* us, so we feel more comfortable with you. Some directors don't like actors." I took that as a compliment.

Dave Gerber became one of my favorite producers, and I later worked with him on *Today's FBI*, with Mike Connors, and *Seven Brides for Seven Brothers*. The latter was a television series version of the famous 1954 MGM musical, where the eldest of seven orphaned brothers brings his bride to the family ranch in Northern California. Each episode had at least one musical number written by composer Jimmy Webb. Gerber decided to shoot the whole series in the actual gold rush country around Murphys, California. He had his own farm there and knew the area well. The cast David assembled was filled with actors who were unknown then but would soon be names. Richard Dean Anderson (later the star

Producer Jon Epstein, Martha Raye and JS.

of *MacGyver*) played the eldest brother, and River Phoenix the youngest. I directed the first episode and several others. *Seven Brides* was a joint production of Gerber and CBS, and a lot of network executives came to Murphys for the shoot. They made me nervous, but the show went well. We were all very excited about doing a musical/comedy/drama on a regular basis, but it was not a big smash with the public. The show lasted for only one season and, worse, in the reruns the wonderful musical numbers were often edited out for time.

Halfway through the season, after I was back in Los Angeles, I got a call from David Gerber asking me to come back and do another *Seven Brides*, because he felt that Richard Dean Anderson had lost some of the fire in his performance. I went back to Murphys for another episode, and in this one I was able to cast my friend Brian Kerwin as one of the guest stars. I told Richard nothing about what Gerber had said, but he sparked to the casting of Brian and gave a lively performance. Later, Gerber asked me, "What did you say to him so I can tell the other directors?" It was almost a repeat of our conversation after I directed *McClain's Law*: He was looking for a secret that didn't exist. I told David that it wasn't anything I said, it was my casting Brian Kerwin. I knew Richard was the kind of actor who respond to Brian's talent and rise to his level.

At Universal, I did another movie-of-the-week called *The Gossip Col-*

Sylvia Sidney, JS and Martha Raye.

umnist. It was produced by Jon Epstein, who hired me for the job as he had done on several series. Kim Cattrall of *Sex and the City* fame made her debut in the picture, surrounded by many name actors: Martha Raye, Sylvia Sidney, Bobby Vinton, Jim Backus, Steve Allen, and Betty White.

We had a fairly liberal shooting schedule for this project, and for the most part it went smoothly. I really enjoyed working with Betty and Martha, and reuniting with some of the other actors I had directed in earlier shows. The particular thrill of that show, however, was the chance to work with Sylvia Sidney, a movie star of the thirties who I had admired as a boy.

There was one traumatic moment with Sylvia during *The Gossip Columnist*. Sylvia lived in Connecticut and she had brought her two dogs with her to California. She even brought the dogs to her dressing room. After she had finished filming a big scene one day, she returned to her trailer to find she had left the gas heater on too high. One of her dogs had asphyxiated. My assistant director, Sheldon Shrager, told me the sad news while we were rehearsing a comedic scene with Lyle Bettger. Then Sylvia came to the set because she said she didn't want to be alone. I told her, "Please, sit in my chair." The rest of my cast became very quiet. It was customary for the assistant director to say "roll it" and when the camera got up to speed I would say "action." But instead of saying "roll it," Sheldon broke the silence with "You say it, Sylvia." Sylvia Sidney said "roll it" in a very loud voice. That relaxed everyone and the scene played well.

Another Universal production I directed in the early eighties was a comedy/action hybrid called *Lobo*. Claude Akins played a crooked southern sheriff and Brian Kerwin, the young actor I later used to good effect on *Seven Brides For Seven Brothers*, co-starred as his deputy. They were both splendid actors and, although the series was silly, I enjoyed it. It was similar in tone to *The Dukes of Hazzard*, which I also directed around the same time. *The Dukes of Hazzard* was a successful television show at Warner Bros. I had never worked on it. In their third year of production, the producers changed and Myles Wilder took over. Since I had worked for him successfully on other shows, he hired me for *Dukes*.

The Duke boys were handsome and honest cousins living with their Uncle Jessie on a farm in Hazzard County, somewhere in the South. They drove their specialized souped-up car, the General Lee, very fast through the countryside. It sometimes looked like it was even flying. The conflict was provided by some unscrupulous characters played broadly, but charmingly, by James Best and Sorrell Booke. It had a style all its own and audiences loved it. I did one episode with John Schneider and Tom Wopat, the original stars, and enjoyed it. Then I was asked to direct the episodes with two new hopefuls, who were being groomed to replace Schneider and Wopat because they had requested too big of a raise. Because my reputation with young actors had been firmly established, I was asked to do three episodes with Byron Cherry and Christopher Mayer.

Byron and Christopher were very appealing, but they didn't have the magic that the original Dukes had. Warner Bros gave in and paid the leads what they wanted. There was a second unit that did all of the car chases with stunt doubles. That, to me, was the most visual part of the show. Often these sequences were filmed before the dramatic portions, so I had to stage my scenes to fit into what had already been done. I had run into this before when the director of *My Three Sons* died and I had to finish thirteen episodes which he had started. I didn't feel I was directing the other actors. Their characters were so well-defined that all the director really had to do was tell them where to stand and where to move, if that. Because the show had been running for several years and was a very well-oiled machine when I came on, the director's job on this show was less artistic than on a dramatic show. Like *Sanford and Son* before it, *The Dukes of Hazzard* was not exactly my creative cup of tea, but it was a fun experience that proved to be very remunerative as they still rerun the episodes I directed.

JS, Byron Cherry and Christopher Mayer on *The Dukes of Hazzard*.

Glen Larson was the creator and executive producer of *Lobo*, and he was well-connected with the top brass at Universal. But Larson had a weakness as a producer, which was that he always tried to get more on film than they had in the budget. Often that put pressure on the production staff and the director to finish an impossible schedule on time. Occasionally *Lobo* would have a big guest star and I remember one in

John Schneider and Tom Wopat on *The Dukes of Hazzard*.

particular with Dean Martin called "Dean Martin and the Moonshiners." In the episode, Sheriff Lobo arrests Dean's band to get him to appear at a rally in support of his re-election campaign. The production department let me have several cameras for that episode, because we needed a lot of coverage for some scenes and Dean was at a point in his life where he could not remember his lines very well. He wasn't drinking, but I think the effects of his wild life were taking a toll on him. Fortunately, the film editor made him look good.

Also at Universal, I was assigned to a fascinating program called *Whiz Kids*, about teenagers who used their computers to help reporters and police solve crimes. It was a fascinating show for me, because of the scenes showing the kids' ability to handle their computers. I had no idea what they were doing. In those days, computers were just beginning to become seen in some households. That was in the fall of 1983, and the following spring I got my first Macintosh.

In the summer of 1984, I went back to San Francisco to direct a comedic mystery series called *Partners in Crime*, which was filmed entirely in the scenic Bay Area. Lynda Carter (from *Wonder Woman*) and Loni Anderson (from *WKRP in Cincinnati*) played women who came from very different backgrounds but had one thing in common: they both had been married to the same private investigator. After he was killed, his will left everything, including his agency, to the two of them. Eileen Heckart, the great stage actress, played their shared mother-in-law. Loni and Lynda, both established TV stars, could be competitive. They would try to outdo each other in the make-up room, which created delays for the crew. It didn't take long to find the solution to that: I told Lynda and Loni that we were going to lose the sun before we could get their close-ups. That got them onto the set in a hurry. Apart from that, they worked hard and both were very professional. It was impossible not to like them.

During the following summer, I enjoyed a splendid vacation in Vancouver, the Canadian city that was becoming a hub of "runaway production." Columbia Pictures asked me to handle the beginnings of a new comedy series based on the successful Richard Pryor / Gene Wilder film *Stir Crazy*. The scripts, by Bruce Jay Friedman, were quite funny, but the casting of two unknowns (Joe Guzaldo and basketball star Larry Riley) in the leads was unfortunate. They lacked the charisma of the movie's stars. However, Canadian crews were good, and we cast some actors locally as well. The locations were more than photogenic, especially the otherworldly Victoria Island.

James McAdams was a producer who I had known since he was an office boy at Universal in the early sixties. Since then he had become a successful producer there, overseeing *Kojak* and *The Virginian*, among others. I had worked with him several times and, in 1985, he called me to New York, where he was putting together a new series with the exciting English actor Edward Woodward. This was *The Equalizer*, a crime show about a polished but deadly vigilante that became a hit for CBS. I liked working with Jim, who had assembled a very professional crew. A director's standard contract provided for advance preparation, but that was ignored in this case because Jim was trying to improve the early scripts.

My episode of *The Equalizer* surrounded Woodward with some wonderful actors, including Christine Baranski and Jim Dale. But it also presented challenges on all fronts. I found a wonderful young man for the guest lead, but I learned on the morning of the shoot he was an understudy in a Broadway show and had to perform that night. His replacement was a young man named Adam Horowitz, who had not acted before but was well-known as a member of the musical group the Beastie Boys. Adam took a great deal of my time on this tricky script which kept having new pages and changes even after we started shooting. I usually had a pretty good working relationship with most cameramen, some better than others, but no one was more difficult than *The Equalizer's* Alan Metzger. He did very good camera work, but our chemistries didn't gel. Despite my close relationship with McAdams and my splendid relationship with Woodward I was never hired for the show again.

My next job was back in Hollywood, on a silly comedy series called *Sledge Hammer!*. It was a parody of the *Dirty Harry* films, with loose-cannon cop Sledge causing mayhem and terrorizing citizens while his female partner, played by Anne-Marie Martin, usually solved the crimes. David Rasche was very funny in the title role, and I thought my first episode turned out well. *Sledge Hammer!* was produced by my old friend Bill D'Angelo, with whom I had worked with on *Batman* and *Alice*, but Bill's boss was the creator of the show, Alan Spencer. I didn't get along with Spencer, who was inexperienced as an executive producer. He didn't seem to know what he wanted and he raised some objections to what I did. At his insistence, I was paid off and let go from the second episode I was supposed to direct.

The last television show I directed took me back to Canada, but this time to Toronto, where television production was flourishing. Vancouver had felt like a semi-rural vacation spot, Toronto was more like a little New York City. The series was *Kay O'Brien*, a sort of light-hearted version of *Dr. Kildare* about a young female physician working in a Manhattan hospital. Patricia Kalember, who played the title role, had refused to cut her hair short, and I remember thinking it too long for a doctor in an operating room. She was a competent actress, but didn't sparkle. The men in the company included Brian Benben, soon to star in *Dream On*, and the distinguished stage actor Jan Rubes. (Rubes had been married to an actress I had worked with in radio, Susan Douglas, and one of their sons had aspirations of becoming an actor. I had given him his first job in Los Angeles.) The producer of *Kay O'Brien* was my old friend and neighbor, Bill Asher, who had produced and directed *Bewitched* and married and divorced its star, Elizabeth Montgomery, since I last worked for him. I enjoyed the series, but *Kay O'Brien* died after thirteen episodes.

You may have noticed some patterns in my work during the eighties: good experiences on shows that got cancelled too soon, and brief stints on more successful shows where, unhappily, I clashed with the producing teams. It had been a while since I had connected with a show like *Naked City* or even *The Bing Crosby Show*, where I loved the material and the people I got to work with. By the middle of the decade, I was beginning to wonder if it was time to retire. The Directors Guild of America, of which I am a member, provides a monthly pension for members of a certain age, and has also fought over the years to secure residual payments for directors whenever their work is repeated or shown in new media. In countries like Spain and Poland and the Netherlands, many of my shows still seem popular, and I still receive a check whenever one of them is broadcast somewhere in the world. The residuals for television programs from my day are much less than the residuals for contemporary television (because directors' salaries have increased dramatically as well), but they are still a pleasant supplemental income. The clincher came when I received an offer on my house in Los Angeles that represented a huge profit. I decided that it was time to stop directing television, to spend some time traveling, and to move back to my wonderful hometown of New York, New York.

I also decided to pursue my dream of directing plays, although luck was not with me. My old friends Jerome Lawrence and Robert E. Lee, the creators of *West Point* back in the fifties, had become very successful playwrights after *Inherit the Wind*, their script about the Scopes Monkey Trial, became a hit Broadway play and movie. Now they had decided to put on a production of *Inherit the Wind* in an actual courtroom in Los Angeles, and asked me to direct. I put off my travel plans and began pre-production work.

Gordon Davidson, then-head of the distinguished Center Theatre Group, was going to supply the nineteen-twenties costumes and other production needs, and the agent Leonard Grant began raising the financing. Unfortunately, the money fell through and the show never happened. After I moved to New York, I was able to direct some staged readings. My old friend, the agent Flora Roberts, introduced me to Andre Bishop, then-head of Playwrights Horizons. This was a highly esteemed group which produced new plays, and for them I directed two readings of new, full-length works. One was by the stage and television actor Scott McKay (who died shortly afterward), and the second was by veteran comedy write Cy Howard. I hoped that the staged readings would lead to a job directing a Broadway play, something I had dreamed of doing for decades. But

Andre Bishop moved on to a more important role, as Artistic Director of the Lincoln Center Theater, and my connection to Playwrights Horizons was severed. I still haven't directed a play in New York City. But there is still time.

Epilogue

"James Sheldon comes from that live/film-New York/ Hollywood period of American TV generally referred to as the 'golden age' of Television. He spent almost a decade working among the prestigious playhouses, and had opportunities to work with some of the best TV talents and early-film series — with Robert Montgomery and Dick Powell, who were actively producing some of the most interesting TV of the period, and the Mr. Peepers *series, remembered, perhaps, more affectionately, by the generation that grew up with the Wally Cox show. It is in Sheldon's early TV work that the real fruits of his talent lie; the period from '60 to '65 reflects an area of accurate evaluation on the Sheldon tele-film. The* Owen Marshalls, Petrocellis, *and* Ellery Queens, *despite their own qualities, are really no more than distant echoes of the work Sheldon was doing some ten years before."*

That's what the critics Christopher Wicking and Tise Vahimagi wrote about me in their book *The American Vein* (New York: E.P. Dutton, 1979). It is one of the few attempts at serious criticism of my work that I have come across. And while I appreciate their generally favorable opinion, and I agree with some of what they wrote, Messrs. Wicking and Vahimagi did not get it completely right. It is true that many of my strongest television programs fall between 1960 and 1965; I have written more about the nineteen-sixties in this book than about any other decade. But I feel that I have been consistent as a director from beginning to end — from *We, the People* all the way to *Sledge Hammer!*.

I don't think my talents or my method of working changed during the remainder of my career. "A director is as good as his tools," the saying goes. I think the scripts in the 1960s that I was hired to stage were better than subsequent scripts. I think the writers of *Naked City, Route 66, The*

Fugitive and *The Millionaire* were better suited to making a director look good. And I think one of the reasons for this was the fact that the producers of those individual shows had more say on the final script. As electronic tape changed the business in the 1960s and sponsors found they could sell all their product with a one minute commercial, producers lost creative control to the networks. By the 1970s, the networks' increased control over the shows, and the desire to reach even larger audiences, flattened out the creative urge. Today's billions of viewers give credence to this flattening. Fortunately, the cable channels offer us *Mad Men* and other ground-breaking shows.

And still the technical side of the business is constantly changing. And the method of distribution still is constantly changing. Today people watch content on the iPod and iPad instead of their televisions, and I predict that those will be replaced with another remarkable invention in a short span of time. Many of the programs I directed, some thirty and forty and more years ago are constantly being rerun. Audiences still want to be entertained and they still like the quality of the shows I did so many years ago. Residually speaking, I am, of course, delighted. At ninety years old, I look happily forward to tomorrow's entertainment technologies.

Appendix

TELEVISION SHOWS

1948   *We, the People*

1950   *Don Ameche's Holiday Hotel*

1951   *Schlitz Playhouse*

1952   *Studio One*
          Robert Montgomery Presents
          Philco Goodyear Playhouse
          U.S. Steel Presents: Theatre Guild on the Air
          Mister Peepers

1953   *Armstrong Circle Theatre*

1954   *Modern Romances*

1955   *Front Row Center*
          Studio 57
          Jane Wyman Presents The Fireside Theatre

1956   *Dr. Christian*
          Celebrity Playhouse
          Ford Theatre

1957   *The Court of Last Resort*
            Dick Powell's Zane Grey Theater
            The Millionaire
            Gunsmoke
            Harbor Command

1958   *Richard Diamond, Private Detective*

1959   *Goodyear Theatre*
            Black Saddle
            Westinghouse Desilu Playhouse
            Law of the Plainsman
            Brenner
            Death Valley Days

1960   *The Donna Reed Show*
            Perry Mason
            87th Precinct

1961   *Angel*
            Target: The Corrupters
            The Twilight Zone
            Route 66

1962   *Margie*
            Alcoa Premiere
            Naked City
            The Virginian
            Espionage
            The Defenders
            The Nurses

1963   *Alfred Hitchcock Presents*
            The Fugitive

1964   *The Bing Crosby Show*
            Bert Lahr Pilot *(Thompson's Ghost)*

1965	*The Patty Duke Show* *The Trials of O'Brien* *My Mother the Car* *O.K. Crackerby!*
1966	*Batman* *Family Affair* *Walt Disney's Wonderful World of Color*
1967	*My Three Sons* *Petticoat Junction* *The Man from U.N.C.L.E.* *Felony Squad* *Ironside* *That Girl*
1968	*Julia*
1969	*To Rome with Love* *My World and Welcome to It*
1971	*Longstreet* *Room 222* *Insight*
1972	*Anna and the King* *Love, American Style* *M*A*S*H*
1973	*Bridget Loves Bernie*
1974	*Owen Marshall: Counselor at Law* *Doc Elliot* *Apple's Way* *Petrocelli* *McMillan & Wife*
1975	*Sanford and Son*

1976	*Good Heavens*
	McDuff, the Talking Dog
	Monster Squad
	Mr. T and Tina
	Alice
	Rich Man, Poor Man — Book II
	Family
1977	*James at 15*
	The Love Boat
1978	*Switch*
	What Really Happened to the Class of '65
1979	*Flying High*
	The Misadventures of Sheriff Lobo
1980	*The Contender*
	Knots Landing
1981	*240-Robert*
	The Waltons
	Nurse
	Code Red
	McClain's Law
1982	*The Dukes of Hazzard*
	Seven Brides for Seven Brothers
	Cagney & Lacey
1983	*Small & Frye*
	Whiz Kids
1984	*Jessie*
	Partners in Crime
1985	*The Equalizer*

1986   *Sledge Hammer!*
Kay O'Brien

TELEVISION MOVIES

1970   *Gidget Grows Up*

1978   *With This Ring*

1980   *The Gossip Columnist*

Index

Abbott, George 50, 57
Adler, Stella 57, 69, 88
Aherne, Brian 72, 82
Albert, Eddie 46-47, 52, 74, 134
Alcoa Premiere 97, 98-99
Alda, Alan 128-129
Alfred Hitchcock Hour, The 98
Alfred Hitchcock Presents 6
Alice 130-131, 147
Anderson, Richard Dean 141-142
Andrews, Dana 98-99
Anna and the King 128, 129
Apple's Way 125, 128
Appointment with Life 66
Armstrong Circle Theatre 5, 53-54, 58, 59, 72
Arnold, Danny 114-115
Asher, Bill 82, 147
Atta Girl, Kelly! 112, 125
Aumont, Jean-Pierre 38-39

Bailey, Pearl 131, 133
Ball, Lucille 108, 131
Batman 6, 102, 112-113, 121, 130, 147
Baxter, Meredith 131, 132
"Bells of Cockaigne, The" 53-54
Bell Telephone Hour 64
Benny, Jack 21, 73, 84
Benson, Leon 75, 78
Berle, Milton 33, 131
Bewitched 42, 82, 92, 111, 147
Bing Crosby Show, The 107-110, 148
Bishop, Andre 148, 149
Boyer, Charles 25, 31-33, 74

Brando, Marlon 37, 43, 88
"Brazen Bell, The" 99
Brenner 100, 132

Bridget Loves Bernie 131, 132
Broderick, James 100, 132
Brodkin, Herb 100-101
Brooks, Geraldine 59, 69
Burns and Allen 21, 73
Bus Stop 58, 76
Buttons, Red 45, 46

Cagney & Lacey 6, 119, 137-138
Carousel 12, 47, 52
Carroll, Diahann 6, 113
Carson, Johnny 71-72, 86
Cattrall, Kim 140, 142
Celebrity Playhouse 81
Champion, Gower 84-85
Champion, Marge 84-85
Cherry, Byron 143, 144
"Chinese Sunset, The" 96
Christian, Linda 24, 25
Cline, Henry 66-67
Clurman, Harold 57-59
Code Red 139
Coe, Fred 37-39, 41, 42, 47, 54, 76, 103
Come Back to Sorrento 83-84, 95
Cooper, Jackie 53, 83
Cooper, Melville 47, 62
Corey, Wendell 51-52, 78-79
Cornell, Katharine 57, 72
Cornfield, Bernie 121-122
Courtland, Jerome 58, 76-77

Cox, Wally 12, 39-43, 151
Cramer, Douglas 94, 131-132
Crimes of Carelessness 12, 67, 69, 139
Cristobel 115
Crosby, Bing 6, 22, 36, 100, 107-108-110, 111, 112
Crosby, Gary 107, 109

Dallas 77, 133, 134
Daly, James 49, 96, 119
Daly, Tyne 96, 119, 137
D'Angelo, Bill 94, 121, 130, 147
Deacy, Jane 37, 54, 76, 77, 84, 125
Dean, James 6, 11, 12, 37, 50, 53-54, 125, 129-130
"Dean Martin and the Moonshiners" 145
Death Valley Days 86-87, 97
Defenders, The 100, 138
Dempsey, Jack 24, 26
Dennis, Sandy 95-96, 102
Desilu Playhouse 83, 95
Diller, Barry 119, 120-121
Disney, Walt 112, 115
Doc Corkle 43
Doc Elliot 6, 127-128
Donna Reed Show, The 82, 96, 120
Dozier, William 45, 48, 59, 73
Duke, Patty 103-104
Dukes of Hazzard, The 6, 143-144, 145
Dunn, James 52, 69

Eastwood, Clint 76-77, 81
"Echo of a Nightmare" 95
Eddie Albert Show, The 46-47
87th Precinct 97-98, 99
Ellery Queen 130, 151
Epstein, Jon 79, 88, 125-126, 129, 134, 141, 142
Equalizer, The 6, 146-147
Erickson, Rod 17, 21, 31, 68
Espionage 100-101

Family 6, 131, 132
Family Affair 116-117
Farrell, Mike 128, 129

Fedderson, Don 85, 95, 115-116, 117, 121
Felony Squad 117
Finian's Rainbow 12, 22
Fonda, Henry 74, 87
Fontaine, Joan 107, 108
Ford Theater 41, 81, 82
Forsythe, John 117, 132
Four Star Playhouse 74
Franciscus, James 127-128
Franz, Adele 51, 71
Franz, Arthur 51, 71, 81
Freeman, Leonard 101, 103
Front Row Center 72
Fugitive, The 6, 14, 84, 95-96, 119, 132, 152

Gallagher Goes West 112
Garland, Judy 70, 71
Garner, Peggy Ann 69, 75
"Gathering Night, The" 48
Gerber, David 94, 139-140, 141-142
Giant 54, 129-130
Gibbs, John 48, 49
Gidget Grows Up 119-120
Gless, Sharon 119, 137-138
Goodyear Theatre, The 115
Gossip Columnist, The 140, 142-143
Graham, Irvin 36, 85
Gunsmoke 5, 117, 140

Haggott, John 47, 49
Hagman, Larry 77, 133, 134
Harbor Command 51-52, 78-79
Hart to Hart 134
"Harvest" 50, 54
"Highest of Prizes, The" 102
Hill, Arthur 95, 112, 125
Hitchcock, Alfred 49, 98
Hoffman, Dustin 6, 103
Holiday, Billie 27-33
Holiday Hotel 5, 34, 35-36, 42, 45, 85
Houghton, Buck 72, 91, 92
Hudson, Hal 72, 73
Hudson, Rock 6, 12, 54, 82, 129-130
Hylands, Scott 132-133

I Dream of Jeannie 77, 111
I Love Lucy 71, 82, 113
"Interrogation" 74
Ironside 6, 113-114
Irving, Richard 73, 99
"I Sing the Body Electric" 94
"It's a Good Life" 91, 92, 94

James at 15 6
Jane Wyman Presents the Fireside Theater 73, 82
Janssen, David 95-96
Jones, Anissa 116-117
Julia 113

Kantor, Leonard 83-84, 96
Karloff, Boris 25, 27, 28
Kaufman, Millard 72-73
Kay O'Brien 147
Kazan, Elia 54, 57, 69, 99
Keith, Brian 53, 116
Kern, James 115-116
Kerwin, Brian 141-142, 143
"King in Yellow, The" 47
"King Stanislaus and the Knights of the Round Stable" 85
Kipling, Rudyard 47, 48
Knots Landing 6, 133-134

Lahr, Bert 110-111, 112
Landis, Jessie Royce 49, 50
Larch, John 85, 92
Laurents, Arthur 58-59, 72
Lawrence, Jerome 75, 88, 148
Leachman, Cloris 92, 98
Lee, Robert E. 75, 148
Levy, Ralph 19, 21, 37, 73, 84
Listening Post, The 66-67, 69
Lobo 143, 145
Lockhart, Gene 53-54
"Long Distance Call" 92
Lorne, Marion 41, 42
Lottery 139
Love, American Style 6, 126
"Love and the Cozy Comrades" 126
"Love and the Mail" 126

"Love and the Mind Reader" 126
Love Boat, The 6, 126, 131-132, 133
"Love Story" 72
Lubitsch, Ernst 35, 61, 87
Lunt (Alfred) and (Lynn) Fontanne 57, 62

MacMurray, Fred 115-116
Mad Men 88, 152
Margie 96
Man from U.N.C.L.E., The 6, 117
Mann, Delbert 37-38
Martin, Mary 24, 26, 77
Martin, Quinn 79, 83-84, 95
*M*A*S*H* 6, 14, 128-129
Matthau, Walter 49-50
Mayer, Christopher 143, 144
McAdams, James 146, 147
McClain's Law 140, 142
McClure, Doug 99, 117, 118
McDuff, the Talking Dog 133
McLean Stevenson Show, The 129
McMillan & Wife 84, 129
Meisner, Sanford 72, 92, 119
Melchior, Lauritz 24, 61
Merman, Ethel 57, 77, 78
Millionaire, The 84, 85-86, 92, 95, 115, 152
Mister Peepers 5, 11, 39-43, 45, 46, 48, 50, 71, 76, 115, 151
Modern Romances 58, 59
Monster Squad 133
Montgomery, Elizabeth 42, 49, 82, 147
Montgomery, Robert 48-53, 82, 151
"Mud Nest, The" 101
Mumy, Billy 91, 92, 93, 94
"My Little Girl" 52
My Mother the Car 6, 113
My Three Sons 5, 97, 115-116, 143
My World and Welcome To It 115

Naked City 6, 9, 12, 85, 96, 97, 102-103, 120, 148, 151
Newman, Paul 6, 49, 54
Newmar, Julie 102, 113
Nurse 138
Nurses, The 97, 100

O.K. Crackerby 113
Orenstein, Bernie 126, 127
"Other Side of the Mountain, The" 95-96
Our Town 54, 58, 62
Owen, Ethel 67, 69
Owen Marshall, Counselor at Law 6, 95, 125-126, 129, 151

Palmolive Party 65
Partners in Crime 146
Patterson, Neva 21, 127-128
Patty Duke Show, The 103-104
Paul Whiteman's Goodyear Revue 5
"A Penny For Your Thoughts" 92
Perkins, Anthony 49-50, 73, 74
Perrin, Nat 71, 72, 86-87
Perry Mason 6, 113
Petrocelli 130, 151
Petticoat Junction 6
Philco/Goodyear Playhouse 37-38, 47
Police Story 139-140
Powell, Dick 74, 151
Power, Tyrone 24, 25
Priestly, Jack 62, 102
Professional Father 59, 71
Proser, Monte 35, 36

Randall, Tony 42-43, 115
Raye, Martha 141, 142
Reagan, Ronald 82, 86-87
Reed, Robert 100, 138
Remick, Lee 6, 52, 53, 83
Remick, Pat 52, 53
Reynolds, Gene 121, 129
Richard Diamond 5, 95
Robert Montgomery Presents 48-53, 58, 59, 72, 75, 79, 82, 83, 96, 119, 121
Rodgers and Hammerstein 47, 52
Rodgers, Richard 25, 27, 34, 35, 52
Rogers, Wayne 128, 129
Room 222 6, 12, 119, 120, 121, 130
Rosenzweig, Barney 137-138
Rosner, Rick 138-139
Route 66 6, 9, 12, 101-102, 103, 125, 130, 151
"Running Scared" 96

Safier, Gloria 43, 49
Salkow, Irving 97, 101
Salmi, Albert 58, 130
Sanford and Son 5, 127, 144
Schneider, John 143, 145
Scott, George C. 99-100, 104
Serling, Rod 91-92
Seven Brides for Seven Brothers 140-141, 143
"17th of June, The" 51
Seymour, Dan 23, 25
"Shadow of a Man, The" 48
Sheldon, Eleanor 12, 82, 83, 87, 107
Sheldon, James, Jr., 12, 47, 107, 121
Sheldon, Tony 12, 82, 107, 121
Sidney, Sylvia 142-143
Sinatra, Frank 54, 69, 84
Sledge Hammer! 147, 151
"Soliloquy" (song) 47, 52
South Pacific 24, 26
Spelling, Aaron 131, 132
Stanwyck, Barbara 69, 74-75
"Steady Man, The" 51
Stern, Joanne Melniker 12, 74-75
Stevenson, McLean 128, 129
"Still Valley" 94
Stritch, Elaine 58, 104
Stroock, Gloria 12-13, 69
Studio 57 73
Studio One 5, 47-48, 50
"Such a Busy Day Tomorrow" 52
Swanson, Gloria 24, 26, 27, 29
"Sweet Charlie" 82
Swift, David 41, 42, 43
Switch 134, 137
Swit, Loretta 119, 129, 137

Target: The Corrupters 101
Taylor, Elizabeth 72, 130
That Girl 5, 114, 126
Theatre Guild On The Air 49-50
There's One in Every Family 46
Thompson's Ghost 110-111
Tobias, Rose 100-101
Today's FBI 140
"Too Young To Know" 67

To Rome With Love 117
Toscanini, Arturo 49, 64
Tracy, Mrs. Spencer 19, 33
Tree Grows in Brooklyn, A 52, 69
Trials of O'Brien, The 103-104
Trotter, John Scott 107, 108
Turtletaub, Saul 126, 127
Twilight Zone, The 6, 11, 91-94, 96
240-Robert 138-139
"Two People" 53

Unger, Maurice "Babe" 75, 79
U.S. Steel Hour 49, 50

Valente, Renee 120-121
Valentine, Karen 119-120
Van Patten, Dick 37, 128, 132
Van Patten, Vince 125, 128
Virginian, The 5, 14, 97, 99-100, 101, 104, 114, 117, 118, 119, 146
Von Stroheim, Jr. Erich 77-78

Wagon Train 5, 97
Walt Disney's Wonderful World of Color 6, 112
Waltons, The 6, 127, 138
Ward, Burt 112-113
Welles, Orson 18, 36, 103
West Point Story 6, 12, 58, 75-78, 79, 134, 148
We, the People 17-33, 35, 37, 68, 73, 84, 128, 151
White, Betty 130, 132, 142
Whiz Kids 145-146
"Whole Truth, The" 92
Who's Afraid of Virginia Woolf? 104, 125
Wiest, Dwight 18, 23, 31
With This Ring 132
Woodward, Edward 146, 147
Wopat, Tom 143, 145

Zane Grey Theater 73

Bear Manor Media

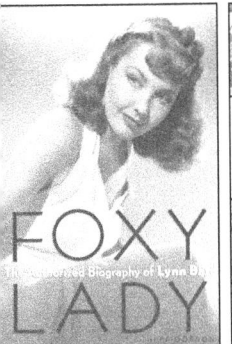

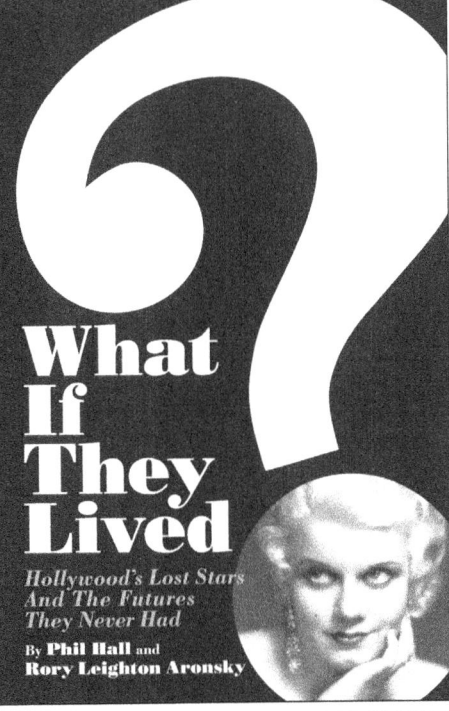

Classic Cinema.
Timeless TV.
Retro Radio.

WWW.BEARMANORMEDIA.COM

www.ingramcontent.com/pod-product-compliance
Lightning Source LLC
Chambersburg PA
CBHW051105160426
43193CB00010B/1318